CONTENTS

Title Page

Copyright

Dedication

Epigraph

Preface

I Was Wrong   1

Hospital Bags   9

March 17, 2020   11

Hush   22

You Will Miss This   51

What is a Week-end?   56

Parental Leave   59

You Can't Say That   66

Just Eat   76

Do You Get It Now?   87

The Sink Caddy   92

Hysterical   98

Vasectomus	107
Bedtime Bullshit	112
Jekyll and Hyde	121
Rage, but Self-Care	125
Popcorn	139
The Kids are Alright?	143
Kindergarten	152
Sliding Doors	159
Epilogue	167
Acknowledgements	171
About The Author	173
Books By This Author	175
Praise For Author	177
What You Won't Remember	181

PREFACE

March 2022

Dear Boys,

After my first round of parenthood, I truly didn't know if I had it in me to survive it all over again. Despite Dad and I always discussing that we wanted two children, it took me a very long time to even consider a potential second child. I wrestled with the idea profusely, and it kept me awake at night for months on end. At one point, I had even told Dad that I was done. I wasn't sure if I could go through another round of morning sickness and didn't believe I would make it out after another bout of postpartum depression.

I had always wanted two children so that if anything ever happened to me or your Dad, you at least had each other in childhood. When I sat at the dinner table, I always felt like there was an empty chair that needed to be filled. I don't have that feeling anymore now that you are both here. I decided I wanted to have another child, even after everything that I had gone through the first time, but I also gave myself time and grace to get there. There was an extra gap year between you and your brother than I had originally wanted, but I needed that year for myself. To heal. To cope. To learn how to be okay with just being okay.

Eventually, I had put in enough hard work to get myself to the point where I felt I was mentally and physically safe and strong enough to take on another pregnancy and child. The pregnancy was difficult again (seriously, is no one working on a cure for morning sickness?). However, I was elated at having a second chance to enjoy the first year of my baby's life, which depression had robbed me of the first time. All I had to do was make it to spring break, and I would be on maternity leave. With a due date of April 4, 2020, I was all set for my redemption with you both.

Then, the world stopped.

Here's what you won't remember.

Love,
Mom

I WAS WRONG

My older son was 22 months old when I found out that I was pregnant again. We explained to him that Mommy was going to have a big belly soon and another baby. He didn't really get it, nor do I really think he cared. My older son, surprisingly, was not possessive of things (at the time). So, we tried to get him as ready as possible for the usurper that was about to come into his life, and he honestly took most of it with grace. There were a few things that my husband and I were adamant about being on top of prior to the baby coming. I will maintain that the newborn phase is hell. Are they snuggly and do they smell amazing? Yes. Do they generally stay in the one spot that you leave them? Yes. What I was wrong about, though, was that once you recover from one phase of hell, a fresh new one shows up in its place. Enter the toddler.

I know there is a strategic sequence of events as to how a child is to move from a crib to a bed. To be honest, I find the multitude of steps that we are supposed to do for everything super tedious and even kind of insulting to kids. I think toddlers are capable of growing up a little bit more gracefully than we think they can. As the new baby was coming, we were not going to buy a new crib since my older son was going to be two and a half when his brother arrived. I know most recommendations suggest that a child should move to a big bed when they are three, but my older son was never a crazy sleeper. He was an asshole-sleeper as a baby, but he never thrashed wildly in his crib, jammed his limbs out between the bars or generally moved at all. A month or so prior to moving him out of his crib, I started putting a pillow in his crib with him. He just threw it around the first few nights, until one night, while watching him on the monitor, he just tucked it under his head and started using it like everyone else. The second adjustment was getting him out of the sleep sack. This one was a little bit trickier. We moved my son in November, so it was already cold enough at night that he needed to be covered. One night, I just decided he was done with sleep sacks. I put one blanket in his bed, and he kicked it off. We made sure he was wearing super warm, fuzzy pajamas because we had foreseen where this was going. I would go in while he was asleep and re-cover him, and in the morning, a portion of the blanket was still on top of him. Success!

Once we let familiarity of his new accessories percolate in his consciousness and crib, we decided that one day, we were just going to move him to his new bed. He sleeps in a daybed, so he has three wooden frames around him. We attached a guard rail on the only open side of the bed, and that was it. The first night that we tucked him in, we explained that he was going to sleep in the new bed. We left the room and watched him on the monitor. He just sat up in bed and looked around his room. He did that for a few minutes, and then he lay down and went to sleep. There were no disasters or tantrums. Honestly, moving my kid to a big bed was the easiest transition of all the transitions we underwent with my oldest. Potty training was a completely different story.

I was not prepared for how disgusting potty train-

ing is. I know that you think you've handled everything gross that can come out of another human
being's body as a parent, but I was wrong. I had
been puked on (partially in my mouth), peed on,
and literally caught shit in my hand, and none of
that prepared me for potty training.

I did all the things that you are supposed to do.
We had a potty in our bathrooms, and we would
often talk to my son about it and have him sit on
it for practice. We read him books about annoying
children who were so eager to use the potty because it meant that they were big and apparently
only needed to have one accident to get it. We
also bought him cool underwear with his favourite characters and machines on them. My husband
had a Friday and a Monday off one weekend, so
we decided that weekend was going to be "booty
boot camp." We were going to put him in underwear and let him frolic about his day while leaving
the potty out in the middle of the living room. We
had agreed that we were just going to stay home
that weekend without leaving the house in order
to optimize the number of opportunities he had to
practice going to the washroom. We didn't make it.
We couldn't stand being in the house for that long,
and by Sunday, we cracked. We begged my mother
to come over for a few hours, and we went to the
movies as a break. We were going stir-crazy. Retro-
spective irony at its finest.

The first few days, he would generally just pee himself. We would walk him over to the toilet if we noticed he started to twitch or right after he had already peed himself. We would simply say, "pee and poo go in the toilet." He looked at me as if I might have been speaking to him in another language. Eventually, on the second day, we let him sit on the potty while watching his 20 minutes of TV until he would just pee. It was ludicrous how excited we got about someone pissing in a pot. We clapped and cheered, hugged and kissed him as if he had just won gold in the Olympics. Then, an hour later, he would piss himself again. The first time that he crapped on the toilet, I remember almost vomiting when I had to clean it out. You carry the little insert from the potty to the toilet and you turn it over for the majority of it to fall out, but it doesn't. The rest of it just smears all over. Then, you must clean the potty like you are washing a dish. Am I grossing you out yet? That's not even the worst part. The worst part was that my kid shit everywhere other than the toilet for the first few days, including, but not limited to: his underwear, his pants, the kitchen floor, the bathroom floor, our back deck, our area rug (our fault, we should have removed it), and at the park (we flew to close to the sun).

Having to clean human excrement out of the grout

of your kitchen floor is one of the lowest points of parenting. It is disgusting. To those of you who aren't parents, you might be thinking, but you've changed so many diapers, how could that be worse? Here is why it is worse. A diaper is a self-contained entity. Most of the shit is absorbed directly into the diaper, and all you have to do when changing it is wrap the diaper up and wipe the remaining skid marks left behind. Diapers can then be wrapped into neat little packages with enough practice and then shoved into a diaper genie while they await transportation to your outside garbage. With potty training, you are picking up a clump of human crap and moving it from the floor to the toilet. I had to Lysol the crap out of my kitchen floor to get it out of the grout. Eventually, we gave up on the little potty and bought a seat that went directly on our toilet, so we simply wouldn't have to touch his shit anymore. Once we did that, potty training got a little less messy (kind of).

There are so, so many accidents when they are learning, and as much as you want to scream when you have yet to change them again, you must stay calm and patient. I was impressed with how calm I was able to stay. That doesn't mean I didn't snap at certain points. One day, he shit himself three times in 24 hours, and I may as well have been as irate as Ursula right before Prince Eric impaled her with his ship. Just buy multiple pairs of underwear, and if you think you have enough, double it. There will be some pairs that will not be worth saving. They will go directly into the garbage can for their shameful departure. Every time my son had an accident, we would rinse out his underwear and leave it in the bathroom to dry if we couldn't take it to the laundry room right away. At one point, we ran out of places in our bathroom to hang his underwear. There was one hanging on the faucet, multiple ones on the counter, one on the towel rack. We might as well have been at the world's most disgusting flea market. Don't believe any of the promises that you can potty train in one weekend. Yes, they might grasp the general concept of it, but that doesn't mean they still won't have accidents. If they are playing or completely engrossed in an activity, they will not want to pee, and therefore will push their bladder to the absolute limit. Sometimes, they make it. Sometimes, they don't.

One of the articles that I had read about potty training suggested that once you were done with diapers, you were done completely so as not to confuse the child. The same article suggested that you set three alarms during the night to wake yourself up so that you could go into your child's room and wake them to take them to the bathroom. Hard pass. I was five months pregnant while we were potty training, and there was no way I was going to give up sleep for that. Also, have you ever woken up a toddler against their will? It's like dealing with a belligerent drunk who thinks the government is out to get them. We adopted a very simple rule: whenever my son was awake, he wore underwear. We bypassed pull-ups during the day entirely because a pull-up is seriously just a diaper. Then, during naps and overnight, we let my son sleep in a pull-up. He would wet himself during sleep, but we were fine with that while he got better at it during the day ("better" meant only two accidents that day instead of five). Eventually, as he got older, he slowly stopped wetting himself during his naps, so we let him have a test run of naps in his underwear. Then, a few weeks later, he started waking up completely dry in the morning. So, we started letting him sleep in underwear. He has only ever wet his bed twice. I thank God for that profusely because if he was wetting his bed regularly, I would be making him sleep on a shower curtain. Potty training sucks. Anyone who says they enjoyed potty training is a liar. Don't feed me some line about how it was so rewarding to see your little one grow up and learn to listen to his body. You were cleaning shit off the kitchen floor, too, Angela, regardless if you admit it or not. And just when I couldn't be more enraged during one of those accidents, my son would turn around and bend over and ask me to wipe him just as a nagging reminder that I was his bitch.

HOSPITAL BAGS

First kid (took a suitcase):

- Standard period pads
- Two different adorable pajamas for me
- Five different outfits for my baby

- Three newborn hats
- A package of newborn diapers and wipes
- Socks that matched my pajamas
- Slippers for me to walk around the hospital
- Hair ties
- Water bottle
- Phone charger
- Baby swaddles
- Adorable mitts for his little hands
- Nursing bras with bows on them
- Chapstick
- Body wash and shampoo,
- Dress to wear home, as I glided to the car
- Brand new car seat

Second kid (took a backpack from the back of the closet):

- Adult diapers (with flowers on them)
- One pajama set that was mismatched
- Two outfits for my baby
- Hat (ultimately covered with blood)
- A package of newborn wipes and diapers
- Hair ties and chap stick
- Water bottle and phone charger
- One baby swaddle (it had whales on it, I think)
- Forgot the mitts (meh)
- A nursing bra that wasn't painful
- Half a bar of soap (I think it was Dove Men)
- A gaping open robe
- Car seat with Cheerios in it

MARCH 17, 2020

My last day of work was scheduled for Friday, March 13, 2020. I had repeatedly told myself that all I had to do was make it to March Break, and then I was going to be in the clear. I would tie up loose ends at school and planned on leaving the building the way Regina George throws the Burn Book photocopies around the hallway. I was out. My son was already signed up to start preschool in April, as I was removing him from his home daycare for the time being. I was going to have two weeks to myself with no work. And with my son in daycare part-time, I was going to relish it. I had booked a massage, a facial, an appointment for my nails, my eyebrows were going to be woven into a sharp point, and I was getting waxed. I was going to go into labour as bare as a plucked chicken.

I had been following the news of the coronavirus about as much as anyone else probably was at the time. I was aware of it, but it was in Asia, so I wasn't too concerned about it. Even when the first person in Canada tested positive in Toronto, it was someone who had just flown back from Wuhan. I didn't start to get nervous until the first week of March when reports were coming out that the virus was starting to rapidly spread across Europe. I picked up my son from daycare one day, and his daycare provider is Italian. She told me that her mother had passed away in Italy, and I asked if she was going to fly home for the funeral. She told me that she was not allowed to fly to Italy because the borders were closed, as they were dealing with a surge in Covid cases. I distinctly remember saying, "Oh, right, it's really bad there right now, isn't it?" I then got into my car and drove home a little heavier.

Even though spring break in Canada is usually

the second or third week of March, most families now feel like they are entitled to just take a vacation anywhere from January to April, regardless of exams or school. I already had students in and out of my classroom from January up until that very last day of work. They were going to Europe or resorts in the Caribbean or getting off a cruise ship. They all cycled in and out of my room, and no one was too concerned that there was a new virus on the loose. I had already brought hand sanitizer into my classroom that I paid for myself because school boards, shockingly (stated with an eye roll), did not pay for sanitizers prior to Covid. You best believe they do now. I had to fund that for my own room. Since I was pregnant, I had one on my desk and one by my classroom door. I asked the students to sanitize as they came in to protect me during my last trimester, which was during Canada's regular cold and flu season. Most of them were compliant. I'm told that I'm intimidating in my non-mutated state of pregnancy. I'm sure a pregnant Ms. Correia was horrifying.

In those first few days of March, the main thing I remember is the increasing frequency with which I heard about Covid. It is so odd to think of that now, as it is the main event of every news cycle every day, that there was a time when we didn't hear about Covid on our feeds or while driving. I checked the news cycles every morning, and on March 11, 2020, I saw the breaking story—

the World Health Organization had declared that Covid was now a pandemic, saying they were forced into action because of the lack of proper protocols being put in place to combat the virus by national governments. My stomach did a small flip, but then, my first period class was about to rush in, so I closed the tab and released the hounds. I went about my day. We talked about it at lunch in my workroom. That was a Wednesday.

On Thursday, I was curious to see if some kids would be absent for the remaining two days prior to the break. They weren't. We all continued to file into the school, maskless, carefree. Students and other teachers were still talking about where they were going to go for March Break. Then, the government announced that March Break was going to be extended for two weeks past its original date to allow for 21 days to "flatten the curve." I think now of those early mistakes compared to other countries, such as New Zealand, who did so well at the beginning. Our borders remained open, and people left, only to be abruptly told on March 17 that they needed to get home now. Two weeks to flatten the curve also wasn't going to do anything. We needed to be locked down for 28 days, two incubation cycles of the virus. When I say locked down, I mean it. No one needed Starbucks during that time, and yet, somehow it stayed open. Ironically, the teaching staff was informed of this extended break by hoarding us all into the lecture

hall—sixty people strong—and being told that because of a highly contagious virus, schools were
going to be closed for an extra two weeks after
the break. My stomach started to sour. We went
about our day, and then, on the last day before the
break, people hugged me goodbye and told me that
I would be just fine.

My family had planned a small event for me to
celebrate the arrival of the other child on Sunday,
March 15. It was a mini get-together with a few
members of my family. At the time, the guidance
had said that any indoor event was still permis-
sible with less than 50 people. We debated cancelling, but most people informed us that they
still wanted to go. So, we had the event because
we were still following the rules, and therefore
thought everything was okay. There were 12 of us.
Even though no one got sick from the event, in
retrospect, I regret having it, knowing what I know
now. Hindsight's a bitch, sometimes. It was my
first experience of feeling physically awkward in
a public setting (I'm socially awkward, but somehow manage to present myself as a somewhat
composed human being). Even though there was a
circulating virus that we knew nothing about, we
were still all indoors together, but we didn't hug
or kiss each other, and everyone gave each other
space. We honestly looked like a bunch of 14-year-
olds at their first high school dance, just lingering
on the floor without knowing what to do. The day

was done, and we all went home. That was the last event that I had attended. It was the last time I was in a room full of people where we all could laugh with one another, share some food and just be human beings. As much as it should have been cancelled, I relish that last get-together because the humour and love in that room was going to be all that I had to sustain me for the foreseeable future.

March 17, 2020 was when I realized the severity of what was happening. I never have the TV on when my older son is awake, but during his nap, I turned on the news because of what the radio had been discussing. The newscaster had shut off all their background music and sounds and was just speaking in a tone of gravitas. The first time I knew that something momentous was happening was 9/11. However, I was 13, and even though I understood that something big was happening, I didn't fully understand why. That static on the radio with only the monotone voice of the newscaster forced me to realize I was experiencing something else momentous, and this time, I understood it. I remember sitting on my couch. My 37-week pregnant belly was smooshed in my mid-section because I was leaning forward with my hand over my mouth while watching the immediate changes going into effect. Our Prime Minister informed us that the border with the United States was closing, that air traffic was now going to be brought to a minimum and that we were heading into a lockdown. I knew from my studies in history that quarantines are always the way that humanity has dealt with every pandemic, so I wasn't scared of that. I was scared that something I had studied and taught about in history was about to become my everyday life.

I remember starting to cry, and my son kicked me. I wasn't naive enough to think this was going to take two weeks or two months. I knew at that moment it was going to take two years at least. I had just taught about the Spanish Flu prior to leaving for maternity leave. My unborn baby would be two when we would have a semblance of normalcy.

I leaned my head forward to rest it against the palms of my hands, and it all came rushing back. The loneliness, the isolation, the depression. I was going to be robbed again. I wasn't just battling myself this time. I now had children to protect amidst a global crisis. I wish I could say that I became a matron of strength and carried on, but for the first time in my life, I became afraid of what prowled outside my home. I became scared of what loitered in my own house. I frantically wiped down all the light switches and doorknobs in my house every day. I closed the door to the nursery to keep it shut like a vault, lest anything from the outside infect the baby's room. My hands became raw from so much washing and sanitizing. The only place I went after that initial announcement was to my medical appointments. I went for my 37-week appointment, and neither the doctor nor I were wearing masks. I asked my doctor right away what this meant for my pregnancy. He said that based on preliminary information that was coming out of China concerning the effects of Covid on pregnancy and babies, I was far enough along and into the clear in terms of fetal development. Had I been in my first trimester, it might have been a different story. This is before Delta, remember. He informed me of the changes in protocol that were going to be taking immediate effect at the hospital. He said everything with the baby was normal and that I was to go home and stay home. So, I did.

My brain was on hyperdrive, considering every worst-case scenario of what could potentially happen to me, my husband, my son and the other one that didn't even exist in the world yet. As such, my brain became a fog on top of the normally dysfunctional pregnancy brain. If anyone wants to tell you that "pregnancy brain" is not a thing or is just an excuse that women use when they forget things, I have the ultimate pregnancy brain story. When I was 38 weeks pregnant, I went downstairs to put in a load of laundry. My older son had shit in a pair of underwear again, so I was soaking them in the laundry room sink with a plug to keep it from draining. That's the last thing I remember.

I went upstairs and gave my son lunch and then

put him down for a nap. After about two hours had gone by, I remembered that I had a load of laundry in the dryer, so I went down to get it. When I opened the door to the basement, I was immediately struck by how humid it felt. I then turned on the light and froze. The entire basement was flooded. I had left the sink running! I honestly have no memory of not shutting off the faucet. I remember turning the sink on, and then I evidently walked away from it while it was still running. I immediately ran down the stairs and waded through the water to shut off the sink. At first, I thought our water heater had burst, but then, I heard the running water. I had put the plug in the sink to soak my son's underwear, hence why none of the water drained. I stood silently for a moment and surveyed what I had done. The water was about one foot high. My son's toys were floating in the playroom. Water was up on the posts of the bed in the spare bedroom, and the new boxes of diapers that we had just been given as gifts were soaked through. To be honest, I wasn't so much worried about the house as I was the diapers. I was not going to waste those. Turns out it's a good thing they are wrapped in plastic because they were fine and could be saved. When I finally snapped out of what was happening, I yelled for my husband to come down. My husband does not get mad easily or often. I could tell on his face that he was furious, but he never got mad at me. I mean, what was he going to do—yell at his wife who was 38-weeks pregnant and about to give birth during a global pandemic? I had a get-out-of-jail-free card, and he knew it. He told me later that he ended up calling his brother and took it out on him. Apparently, he informed his brother that he couldn't yell at his wife, so he was going to yell at him. So, my brother-in-law sat on the phone for seven minutes and took the verbal lashing for me. My brother-in-law thought it was hilarious. Thanks, buddy. We called my parents who rushed over with a mop (I may have conveniently diminished the amount of water that was in the basement at first). My parents and husband sucked up the water with shop vacs and collected what they could with a bucket and dumped it down the bathtub. My son and I just sat on the steps and watched everyone else clean up. I mostly had to sit with him to stop him from trying to swim in it because he didn't get why everyone was freaking out. He thought it was a pool we had built for him and wasn't impressed that we wouldn't let him run through it like a splash pad. We clearly broke our quarantine, but I'm going to give myself a pass on that since I flooded my fricken basement.

My parents took our area rug with them to dry in their backyard, and we set up fans and dehumidifiers around the basement. The doors wouldn't close because the frames had absorbed so much water, and the baseboards, which had just been installed, were completely damaged and were going to need painting.

As if dealing with a flooded basement wasn't enough, a few days later, my son looked at me with his innocent little eyes and quietly asked, "Mommy, am I bad?" I was caught off guard and simply asked why he would think that. He looked at me and said that no one came to play with him anymore, and he was wondering if it was because he was bad. I cried. I was spiraling. I had lost control of everything around me, and my second kid wasn't even here yet. Within the next week, between 38 to 39 weeks of pregnancy, my husband and I would both get sick (I mean, maybe it was Covid, maybe it was the wading in the water?). It all didn't matter a week later because, like it or not, my doctor told me my baby was coming out early, and I had two days to get ready.

HUSH

The day that my first son was born, there were 11 babies born at the hospital within 24 hours. Apparently, that is a lot. We asked our nurses what the average was, and they said anywhere from four to five babies was a normal day. If only one to two babies were born in a day, it gave them a chance to catch up on paperwork. The fact that there were 11 born that day made for a chaotic maternity ward. I very much remember a lot of the sounds from my first birth. I kept my eyes closed through most of my first labour, so my ears were hyper-aware of my surroundings. The main sound I remember hearing was of the person in the delivery room next to me.

When I first arrived at the hospital, I had to wait in the triage room for a few hours during my labour because there were no birthing rooms available. They were all occupied by other women in labour. After one had been sanitized and readied for me, I moved down the hall and was able to labour with some dignity in private as opposed to the triage room, which constantly had other women in and out. When I moved to the delivery room, the woman in the room directly beside me was screaming. I assumed she was pushing at the time and instantly began to panic that it was going to be me shortly. I proceeded to have my epidural. I vomited a few times, but I didn't scream. The whole time that I was in labour, and then delivered my son, she was screaming. When it was a few hours later, and my parents and in-laws all came to meet the baby, she was still screaming. The hospital was busy. We could hear cheers from the waiting room when a nurse would go out to announce that their new family member had arrived. We heard the patter of siblings coming to meet the new bundle that would dethrone them. We could also hear the nurses talking in the hallway. While

I had my visitors, we overheard one of the nurses say that the woman next door was finally asking for an epidural because she no longer wanted to stick to her birth plan of an unmedicated birth. Everyone in my room took a sigh of relief, not because the sound of her screaming reminded me of *Psycho's* shower scene, but because the poor woman was finally going to get some relief.

Also, just a side note, can we chill on the birth plans a bit? I'm not saying don't make them, but can we all please just remember that the objective that day is, again, to get you and your baby out alive, and you might need to be a little bit flexible on how that happens. If you want to go into birth knowing that you need Enya playing on your Air Pods, take her with you, but you don't get a medal for suffering. I know some people hate that phrase, but it is true. If you want an unmedicated birth, have one, but know that woman and I both left the hospital with a baby on our laps. She wanted to experience birth without medication, and even though I will never understand her desire to do so, I will firmly stand by her choice to try. In return, she does not get to put herself on a pedestal above me because I chose to have a birth that was medicated. If we were both safe, that is what mattered. My sincere hope is that she herself or anyone around her did not make her feel like a failure because she decided to ask for help.

When I was finally able to move to the recovery room, I heard the same woman move into the room next to me. At the time, we were in a private room, but the bathroom was shared between myself and the other mother. First of all, no new mom should be expected to have to share the bathroom after giving birth. It takes a solid 23 minutes to figure out how to go to the bathroom after giving birth and being constantly worried that the person in the room next to you is also going to need to come in for a diaper change (her own, not the baby) is not particularly helpful. The hospital was alive, babies were crying, grandparents were laughing, mothers were screaming, and partners were haphazardly supporting the birther to get a human out of their body.

The only way that I can explain my second birth is the stillness of it. Like the opening credits of a science fiction horror film. If I had to pick a soundtrack to my second birth, it would be "The Sound of Silence" by Simon and Garfunkel. Take a minute and listen to that song. It is eerie, ethereal and very unsettling. It forces you to immediately take notice. That or the soundtrack when all the contestants are going to the game hall in *Squid Game*.

My province went into lockdown on March 17. The fact that I knew I was going to be delivering a baby in two weeks forced a terror into my chest that

I didn't know was possible. My oldest son, who had previously been in daycare until my maternity leave started, was sick. He had a cough and runny nose. He got better, and then a few days later got sick again. I then caught his cold because he repeatedly managed to sneeze into my open mouth when talking. A few days later, my husband also got sick. I was the only one who developed a fever. At that point, when we were ten days into a global pandemic and knew absolutely nothing, I felt the cracks starting. We also had contact with people who had just travelled prior to the pandemic being announced. We did not know what to do. At one point, I called my doctor and asked if I could have a test. I was informed by the hospital staff that tests were only being given to people who had been out of the country for the previous fourteen days. We obviously had not left the country; therefore, we were to assume we had Covid and stay home.

While all of this was happening, I was, of course, 38, and then 39-weeks pregnant. My second pregnancy had been difficult as well but for very different reasons. I had the same raging morning sickness as I did with my first, but this time, it went away after five months as opposed to eight. At one point, I had to do a transvaginal ultrasound. Did you all know that was a thing? There is a wand designed to shoot straight up into your vagina to take a way closer look at your cervix than you would ever want to see. It wasn't even

painful; it was just more awkward to be pene-
trated by a woman with a condom-wrapped wand
while telling you about how she puts sour cream
in her brownie mix to make them extra creamy.
The ultrasound confirmed that my placenta was
partially covering the birth canal. It wasn't completely obstructing it, but it was covering enough
of it that if it didn't move out of the way, I was
going to have a scheduled cesarean in order to
avoid going into labour, which could be very dangerous with a baby who wants to get out but can't
find the exit. Luckily, that fixed itself because my
placenta (and hurdle one) moved out of the way
(good job, placenta). Then, my son decided that
being transverse was cool. It was not. My doctor
gave him a two-week window to see if he would
shift on his own. If he did not figure it out by 36
weeks, I was going to have to go to the hospital to
have the doctor try to manually flip him. Thank-
fully again, this resolved itself, and he put his own
head down. We were able to figure this out because
of an ultrasound to confirm his position. I went in
that day expecting to find out if I was going to need
a cesarean or not, and I got a hell of a lot more than
I wanted.

When I was 36 weeks, I went for that ultrasound to
see my baby's position. Right away, the technician
told me that he was head down. I was getting ready
to be on my way when the technician went very
quiet. She began to furiously take screenshots. She

then excused herself for a minute and left the room. She had locked the screen, so I couldn't actually see the ultrasound pictures. My heart started racing, and I finger painted with the ultrasound jelly on my stomach as a distraction to keep myself from screaming. I was in the room alone because my husband was not allowed to come to the hospital with me due to Covid. When the technician came back in, she informed me that I was going to be moved to obstetrics but did not specify why. As I followed six feet behind her in the hospital, I was trying desperately not to cry. I was handed off to a new nurse who told me she was going to hook me up to a monitor in order to test the baby's heart rate. She took my blood pressure, which was through the roof. Well, no kidding, my baby was undergoing the happy baby test, and no one was telling me why.

I was left in the room for 30 minutes with monitors attached all over my body and a printout of my son's heartbeat slowly spitting out next to the bed. I have never paid attention to the sequence of a line as closely as I had that day. When he wasn't moving enough, I would poke and prod my belly to irritate him into movement. I didn't know what was happening, why I was being told I had to stay at the hospital and why I suddenly had to have his heartbeat checked. Eventually, a very kind obstetrician came in and introduced herself. I couldn't contain it anymore and began to cry. I told her that no one had explained to me why I was moved after my ultrasound and asked if my baby was okay. She explained to me that my baby was in the tenth percentile for weight (an average-sized, healthy-weight baby is a baby at 50%, so the fact that mine was in the tenth percentile meant that he was extraordinarily tiny). My face got hot with tears. I asked her what that meant. She said she was reviewing the ultrasound to check the ratio of the size of his head to his body to rule out macrocephaly. She clearly could tell by the expression on my face that I had no idea what she was talking about. She said that, in certain cases, if the baby's head is drastically larger than the body, as in disproportionate, it means that there is an exorbitant amount of fluid in the baby's skull, which can cause issues with the baby's brain. So, my own brain went into overdrive. She quickly looked over his heartbeat scan, nodded to herself and told me she would be back in ten minutes.

Those ten minutes were the longest ten minutes of my life. I had been told potentially life-altering news without actual confirmation of what was happening. I was completely alone and terrified that every person I encountered was a walking virus. Please remember that, at this point, masks were not mandated. All the hospital staff were wearing them. I also had a mask on at the hospital, because of my cough, but out in the general world, masks were not a thing yet.

When the doctor finally came back in, I could tell she was smiling because of her eyes. I thank the universe every day for that smile. She told me that in testing out the ratios, my baby did not have macrocephaly. His head was proportioned to his body, and all his organs were within the safe range of development. She first asked me how big I had been at birth (six pounds, eight ounces). She then asked me how big my first son had been at birth. When I informed her that he was seven pounds, she clapped her hands together and said, "Well, that's it then." I was about ready to scream at this point until she carried on and explained that I just made small babies. She said it had nothing to do with how much I was eating; my genetic composition was just designed to make tiny humans. She did say, however, that my son's weight was still lower than normal, and as a result, I would likely not go to a full-term pregnancy. It would be safer to get him out through induction whereby my labour would be easier to control. When I asked why, she explained that if I went into labour naturally, the uterine contractions may be too forceful for the baby that it could potentially crush or bruise him because of how small he was. I didn't even know that was a thing. If I was induced, the amount of Pitocin administered could control the frequency of my contractions, and therefore the force being applied to the baby. Additionally, she told me that my amniotic fluid was low, and I was going to have to come back once a week to monitor both his weight and my amniotic fluid volume.

She also told me to manage my stress. During a pandemic. While 36-weeks pregnant. With a two-year-old at home who had become feral because he had not left the house.

Side Note:

When people asked me what I wanted, I always said I just wanted a healthy baby. And I meant it. You don't realize how many issues can happen in a pregnancy until you are tested for them. For every ultrasound, blood test and blood sugar test, I always held my breath while waiting for the technician to turn the screen or for my doctor to explain the results because all I would want to hear is, "everything looks normal." When you don't hear that, your brain goes into panic mode.

In the end, when you do manage to leave the hospital with your baby who is breathing and eating on their own and is safely tucked away into the car seat, there is a moment of guilt. When you have to walk by the NICU and see the parents standing over their child's incubator with a tube feeding them and another keeping oxygen in their lungs, you want nothing more than to run over to those parents and hug them. You want to let that mother's broken body sob into your broken body, and you want to scream and rage and apologize to her for how unfair all of this is. But you don't. You watch silently and thank the universe that your child is okay. You might cry, but then, you pick up your own car seat and send out a prayer of gratitude into the universe that your child is healthy and going home with you. The images of the NICU still haunt me in my dreams, sometimes. I met one mother whose child was in the NICU during my first hospital stay. When I say "met," we didn't have a conversation. We made eye contact with each other, and there was a colossus of understanding in that moment of interlocked silence. I cannot begin to imagine and will never claim to have any firsthand knowledge or experience of the NICU. Parents with such experience, though, are strong because they have no choice but to be so and face a battle you cannot understand without direct experience. It lends honesty to saying that all you truly care about is a healthy baby.

Also, can we please stop it with the gender reveals? I have seen multiple news reports of wildfires being set because of them or people being hurt because an animal was somehow involved. You don't need a dove that is dyed pink to be released into the air while Prince plays in the background or a hot air balloon that turns blue right before bursting into flames. I found out the sex of both of my pregnancies, but that wasn't the original plan. I didn't need it to plan out his nursery. (Don't even get me started on those. Your baby sleeps in pitch black and doesn't care that you painted a mural of the Rocky Mountains behind his crib. They will also puke all over that organic, imported crib you bought from Geneva). I found out the sex because I was so sick with morning sickness in both of my pregnancies that I needed some positive news to get through the rest of it. But seriously, who cares what sex your baby is! Ask the technician if there is a penis or a vagina if you want, call your family and friends, but make sure their organs are developing properly. That's what should matter.

Return To Our Normal Program:

I went home after this and explained everything that had happened to my husband. My own doctor called me the next day to check in on me. He informed me that he had set up a weekly appointment at the hospital for my ultrasounds. He said I was likely within 14 days of giving birth, so I had to quarantine. Please remember that this was in the first two weeks of the pandemic. We didn't know anything really about Covid yet. The only time anyone in my household was allowed to leave the house was when I went to my ultrasound and doctor's appointments. My husband was able to work from home, and my son was pulled from daycare and kept home with us. Thank God I was officially on maternity leave because if I had to work while all of this was going down, I would have had a nervous breakdown. We had family members leave groceries for us at the door. I rallied against an angry two-year-old who didn't understand why he couldn't leave the house. For the first time in his life, I started letting my son watch movies, so I could have an hour and a half to sit on the couch next to him because my swollen body had reached its limit.

I continued going to the hospital for my weekly appointments and began to wear a makeshift mask. These were not mandated yet or available, but I wore what I had. Wearing one was extremely uncomfortable, and I don't mean physically. People stared at me and didn't even try to be discreet about it. It was obvious that they were staring at me. I imagine people either thought I was being paranoid (although my huge belly should have been enough reason for you to give me a pass) or that I was sick. People would purposely avoid me while I walked through the hospital out of fear that I was ill. As I was sick during the last few weeks of my pregnancy, I was considered high-risk for contamination every time I entered the hospital. The nurse who always came to get me for my ultrasound wore what I can only describe as a fishbowl on her head and was covered in gowns and gloves. It was impossible for us to hear one another, but we figured it out. For my final three ultrasounds, I was told that my son was gaining weight, not a ton, but he was stronger. My amniotic fluid was depleting rapidly, though, and he was going to have to come out at 39 weeks before the amount of amniotic fluid loss was dangerous. I know you are probably wondering how the fluid was depleting. The answer to that is simple. It was just leaking out of me. The last few weeks of my pregnancy, it just felt like I had constantly peed myself, which totally happened, too. I dreaded every time that I went to the bathroom because I was terrified to look down and see how much more fluid had come out and was perpetually assessing it to make sure there was no blood in it.

When I was discussing the new procedures for the hospital with my doctor, he informed me that I was only allowed one person in the room with me. That wasn't going to be a problem because my husband was going to be the only one present anyway. My husband had recovered from his cold; however, we did have one problem. My husband has seasonal allergies, which manifest as a cough. Not ideal during a pandemic, which centers on a respiratory virus. My doctor said we would both be screened at the door on my induction date. They obviously couldn't turn me away, but they had a right to turn my husband away. We panicked in those last few days and decided to potentially have my mom go with me, instead, because if my husband was turned away at the door, I was not allowed to call someone else to be with me. We put her on standby. We decided that my husband was going to come with me, and if he was turned away, then I prepared myself mentally for potentially giving birth alone. I wasn't worried about going through the delivery alone. My husband was completely useless during it anyway, and I didn't need my head stroked for encouragement this time. When you need someone is during the aftercare. The nurses are with you through the whole delivery but trying to take care of a newborn while you yourself can barely walk is what gave me pause. We drove to the hospital in silence on March 30, 2020, not knowing what was going to happen. I was terrified of being alone. And my husband was petrified at having to sit at home, not knowing how I was or if our son had been born and if he was okay. I kept concentrating on my breathing to keep myself calm. Ultimately, my husband was able to get medical documents and took all his medications and prescriptions with him, explaining his cough was from his allergies. The hospital staff cleared him to enter with me, and relief washed over both of us. I grabbed his hand and was grateful I wasn't going to be alone. No one who is about to be in the most vulnerable moments of their life should ever have to do that alone.

We walked through the birthing wing, and my husband commented on the fact that the hospital was deserted. I had forgotten that this would be strange for him, because I had already gotten used to the new climate at the hospital from my weekly appointments. He asked if it was always like this, and I said yes. The silence of the hospital was deafening. There were no visitors. No one was sitting in the waiting room. The gift shop had been closed. There was one man that got off the elevator and, when he saw us, purposefully crossed to the other side of the hall. It was a horror film, remember? Something was lurking, and we all knew we were supposed to be scared, but we weren't sure of what exactly. When I asked the nurse what it was like being in the hospital right now, she simply stated, "this is the calm before the storm. This is going to get worse." I inhaled sharply, as what she had said solidified that I was about to give birth at the very beginning of a global pandemic.

Getting induced was an entirely different experience than waiting for natural labour. Some women have negative induction experiences, but mine was positive. Well, mostly. I was able to walk into the birthing suite on my own because I didn't want to rip out my husband's hair while having contractions this time. Not because I was mad at him, just because it would have likely felt cathartic. We were able to unpack our belongings. I changed into my hospital gown comfortably and hung out on the hospital bed, waiting for the nurses to come in. However, because I was sick, I had to deliver in a room with a specific ventilation system just in case what I did have was Covid. It is ludicrous to me now that I was not able to have a test prior to delivery, but because I had not travelled, I was still not eligible for a test in the early days of the pandemic.

I had been sick multiple times during this pregnancy. I was pregnant in fall/winter/spring, and in Canada, we spend three quarters of the year in flu season as opposed to the one season we are not. I remember asking my doctor around five months if there was any cold medication that I could take. He explained to me that it was inevitable that I was going to be sick through the whole pregnancy because I basically had no immune system. He explained that when someone is pregnant, the only way the body sustains the pregnancy is by suppressing the immune system because half of the genetic material in the baby belongs to another human being. By nature, our own immune system would attack the baby in order to protect itself. Mind-blown. It makes sense. Babies are parasites who take everything they need from your body and its reserves without any regard for what that does to its host. I also wasn't expected to wear a mask because I was labouring. My husband wasn't required to wear a mask either, but he was not allowed to leave the room during delivery. Unfortunately, for him, there were no runs to grab a doughnut. He slept through most of my second labour, with my blessing, and I just threw my water bottle at him when I needed something.

I was lucky that I did not have to have prostaglandins shot up my vagina to induce labour. As it was second, my son had already dilated four centimeters on his own. The nurse began the induction process by setting up an IV in my hand so that she could introduce the Pitocin. It began as a steady drip and she asked me to inform her if I started to feel anything. I didn't. She increased the dose. I started to slowly feel the tensing of my abdomen. There really is no way to describe what a contraction feels like. The early ones feel like the worst period cramps you could imagine. The later ones? Oh man. You know when you are carving a pumpkin and trying to get the seeds out, so you have to forcefully dig a spoon into the flesh of the inside of the pumpkin, and then violently scrape all the seeds out repeatedly? It is kind of like that. The inside of your uterus is being forced to eliminate its inner contents, and it's not pretty. Sorry that I just ruined pumpkin carving for you. I felt my first contraction, and then a second one five minutes later. The anesthetist came in shortly after and introduced herself. My mouth must have fallen to the floor because I was shocked that she was going out of her way to come in and ask me if I wanted an epidural. With my first, I was so close to delivery that I was scared I was not going to have one, and here, she was offering one to me on a beautiful platter. She told me she was not at all busy anymore because most surgeries had been put on hold, and so, she was fully committed to the maternity ward. She informed me she had just numbed two women for their scheduled C-sections and had some free time. This was the mother-freakin' jackpot. I told her I was ready for my epidural, and she told me she was going to get her tools and be back in ten minutes. She was back in seven (yes, I counted), and I had to endure one more small contraction while I waited. Then, sweet Mary, mother of bliss was shot into my back, and I had no more pain for the rest of my delivery. When I say none, I mean none. My second delivery was painless. I was in labour for eight hours and felt absolutely nothing. At one point, I told my husband I should have packed the iPad to watch Netflix. I think God thought I was getting a little too cocky.

Since I was induced, my belly was constantly hooked up to a monitor that tracked the baby's heart rate to see how he was handling the forced contractions. This was also necessary because he was so small, and they wanted to make sure he wasn't under severe stress. The nurse came in periodically to check the heart rate monitor, then left to tend to another patient, but it wasn't until one screening that she didn't leave like usual. She lingered silently. There was that chasm of a word again. She never outwardly did anything that led me to believe something was wrong, but if there is one thing you never want to hear from your delivery nurse, it's silence. She left the room, and my doctor came back in with her. They both stared at the monitor. I just stared at my husband, and I snarled at him like a cat to get his attention. The doctor explained that the baby's heart rate had become erratic, and he was struggling with the pressure from the contractions. The nurse told me that I was going to have to change my seating arrangement to try to jostle my son into a position that took some physical pressure off him. This was a little bit more difficult because I had the epidural. I had a misconception that when you have an epidural, you are paralyzed. You're not. You cannot walk because you wouldn't have a sense of your own weight, and therefore would be unstable. However, you are still aware of your legs. They just feel like concrete. You can also still move them slowly. That is the insane part of an epidural. I could still feel my son kick me or turn, and even though I was completely aware of his movements, I was able to feel it all without experiencing any of the pain. I moved from my left side to my right, and I heard his heartbeat drop. The nurse quickly moved me on all fours, using pillows to support my legs because I really couldn't do it myself. My husband supported me because I couldn't feel the lower half of my own weight. The baby did not like that position at all. I was then instructed to sit up in bed, ramrod straight, and place the soles of my feet together in order to open my pelvis. His heart rate steadied. I had to stay like this for an hour. That might not seem like a long time, but when you have a back that's completely worn out from nine months of carrying another human being, being forced to keep it straight is futile. Eventually, his heart rate stabilized, but it was still extremely faint, almost still. My doctor broke my water with the crochet needle (hello, old friend). The first time my water broke, the bed became soaked and needed to be changed. This time, my doctor asked me if I cared about my socks. I said no, and he proceeded to rip my amniotic sac. It was a trickle. He knew since I already had low amniotic fluid that there wasn't much left. With my water broken, we were now on a time limit, and D-Day was coming. His heart rate was monitored, and I laboured for eight hours. I slept through most of it if I'm being honest, and minus the fear of freaking out about his heart rate, it was simultaneously calm and disorienting.

My doctor came in to check my dilation and told me I was at ten centimeters, and he could feel my baby's skull. Go time. My doctor took a stainless-steel bowl and filled it with hot water while the nurses laid out their surgical instruments. I was told to begin pushing. It took nine minutes this time. I'm not saying that because I'm amazing; I'm saying that because he was so tiny that it didn't take as much force to get him out. I pushed three times. In between contractions, my doctor purposefully looked away from my vagina. I appreciate the fact that he was trying to preserve my dignity, but I was so over dignity by this point. We talked about Covid, his own children and how all the nurses had taken bets on whether my socks would be covered in fluid and blood by the end of delivery (they were not, and this is rare apparently, so I hope whoever won the pool felt stellar about their bet). I knew my son was out because I felt the release of his weight from me, but there was a pause and a heavy, unwelcome silence. I didn't look down to see what was happening, but I saw the doctor's arm swoop in between my legs quickly and move in a repeated circular motion. The umbilical cord had been around my son's neck multiple times. It wasn't completely constricting him, but what was happening was every time I had a contraction, the force of my uterus would pull on the cord, and therefore cause it to tighten around his neck and loosen again when the contraction was over. That was why his heart rate was erratic. As soon as I saw my doctor pull up the cord towards him, I heard a gentle smack. And then, I heard my son cry. And I took a breath. Waiting for that cry is the longest moment of a mother's life. He weighed six pounds, five ounces, and even though that is not considered a dangerous weight by any means, he was tiny. The doctor did a once-over and placed him on my chest. My husband cut the umbilical cord, which is kind of like cutting through a sponge. After the initial few cries, newborns generally don't cry for the first few hours of their lives. They make up for this later, but generally they just drift in and out of sleep while you help regulate their temperature by having them skin to skin. Obviously because delivery is an all-hands-on-deck experience, I completely forgot we were in a pandemic for those few hours. It was only after, when I was moved to recovery, that it all came rushing back. The transfer nurse came in and commented on how clean my socks were while she removed my catheter. The socks, really? She then did the ice test by placing blocks of ice on different parts of my leg to ensure I had regained feeling after the epidural. Once I could stand on my own, I was whisked into a wheelchair and moved upstairs. In the long run, those minor scares that we had with my son are nothing in comparison to the health concerns that some babies and their parents immediately face after birth or for those parents who never get to hear their baby cry. My compassion and heart is firmly with those parents fighting a battle I will never understand.

The recovery ward was dark. The main thing I remember is the hum of the ventilation system, which had been mobilized into overdrive because of Covid. There really is no other way to describe it. Just an unsettling stillness while the ventilation bore its constant reminder of the virus. There was no laughter, no crying. The mothers were all spread out in different rooms far away from each other. I never saw another patient the entire time I was in recovery. We felt like we were the only ones in the entire hospital. It was not a good feeling. I will not lie, though. It was a relief to not have visitors. When you have just had your body ripped in half, the last thing you want to do is see people.

I know everyone is so excited to see the baby, but often the mother is forgotten. She, too, has had a traumatic day and is in the midst of processing everything that has happened to her. It was nice to not have to worry about my state of dress because the only people who saw me were my husband and the nurses. The only moment of sadness post-recovery was the absence of my older son. Another moment of silence. I never got to hear the patter of his feet coming towards my room or the sound of his little voice asking his grandmother where his baby brother was. I never got to hear the door squeak open and see his little face light up in wonder as he clumsily climbed up the hospital bed to sit with me and his brother. That picture doesn't exist, and it never will. It wasn't until that moment that it really hit me that I had delivered a child in a momentous event in human history. I had delivered a baby in a time of turmoil and fear, like the women of countless events in history. Women who had delivered their babies in times of war, hunger or oppression. Our children had all emerged into the world in a period of darkness and fragility and yet they had brought with them the chance for light.

One other major difference in my experiences is that with my first son, he was periodically taken out of my room to the nursery. When he had to do bloodwork or when he was being checked by the pediatrician, all of that was done in the nursery.

Also, at one point, the nurses asked if I wanted them to take him out of the room for three hours (but only three hours) because he had to come back to be breastfed. Those three hours when he was out of the room were the only three hours of sleep that I got in a 72-hour period. Sleeping while in labour has an asterisk on it because you are more in a kind of semi-blackout state than a restful state.

I have a problem with the automatic assumption of rooming in. I'm not saying that we should return to our post-WWII dystopia where husbands smoke in the lounge while waiting for their wives who take forever to deliver a baby. I do, however, think there is something to be said for a baby spending some time in the nursery after birth. Both of my sons were given skin-to-skin by both myself and my husband after birth in order to help regulate their temperature in the world. However, the whole idea that after a woman's body has been shredded, she, without skipping a beat, is also left with a new little creature to simultaneously care for lends to the greater idea in our society that the mother is meant to be the entire caregiver to that child, wholly and without reservation. If the baby is kept in the room with the mother, it makes it easier to pick up on her baby's feeding cues in order to facilitate successful breastfeeding. Well, what about mothers who don't want to breastfeed or can't? What if there are multiple children? What about a mother who has just had a cesarean, with a partner at home that is taking care of older children because they don't have any family close by? What about a mom who just wants some uninterrupted sleep because her body was just cut open or torn in half? This push for rooming in, like everything else in motherhood, should ultimately come down to choice. Do I think that at some point an attachment-style parenting pusher, who refers to formula as "the F-word," is going to tell me that my baby is going to hate me when he's 16 because I sent him to the nursery periodically while in hospital? Probably. But my son wasn't breastfed and didn't co-sleep and he used to cry when I had the audacity to use the bathroom because I was away from him for five whole minutes. If my son hates me when he's 16 it is because he's 16, not because I banished him from my sight for three hours of sleep in the first 72 hours of his life. During Covid, this was, of course, different. The baby did not leave my hospital room. All his blood work and pediatric screens were done in the room with me as the only babies allowed in the nursery were the NICU babies requiring specialized care. As a result of this, I was there when the pediatrician ensured my son was okay.

His hips and heartbeat checked out, but then they checked his eyes. At first, the pediatrician kept checking his eyes without success. She tried to move him into different positions, but whatever she was looking for, she was struggling to find. She told me she was going to have to leave the room and come back. That was the only time after my second son was born that I cried. Even my husband told me that I was much more like myself the second time, and I fully believe that that was because I was induced. I was able to get a full night of sleep before I went in, and because I wasn't withering in pain for hours on end, I didn't feel completely emaciated after my second son was born. When the pediatrician left the room, though, I instantly panicked, as I imagine anyone would when they think there's a problem with their child's sight. Eventually, the pediatrician returned with a second doctor, who did a replica of all the same tests that had been done, and he turned to me and said, "we're good, he's fine." Turns out the first doctor's instrument was not working. The thing I was most concerned about after my second birth was the fact that they were not doing hearing tests at the hospital because of Covid. It is so critical for children, even newborns, to begin listening to the world around them in order to help proper speech and communication. Right away, that was not going to be okay with me. When my son was a few weeks old, I immediately began calling around to private hearing clinics to schedule a hearing test for him. I was able to get him into a private clinic, and the test that was done there is the same as the one that is done at the hospital. The only difference is that the test is easier on a newborn because they don't move. The audiologist told me that my son's hearing was cleared and promptly charged me $120 for the three-minute test. I realize that I am lucky and have the means to pay for that test. Public Health contacted me when my son was already six months old, asking if he still needed a test, but by then, it was already too late and would have no doubt already affected his development.

In extreme examples as with a pandemic, there is a justification for having that choice of rooming taken away from mothers; it is in an extraordinary circumstance. Because of the pandemic, I was never going to say to the nurses, "take him away," with a flit of my hand like the Queen, but under normal circumstances, I would have sent my second son away without hesitation. There seems to be this decisive shift after birth, though, that suddenly, the baby becomes the patient and not the mother. The nurses still care for you, check your vitals and feed you, but everything comes down to what the baby needs in those 24 hours of the hospital—not what the mother needs. If you just need a few hours to breathe, ask for your child to go to the nursery, do not feel bad about that. You are entitled to a few hours, my god; you are going to be taking care of that kid for the next two decades. You've earned a few hours.

Upon discharge, we were told to go home and quarantine again. We were on lockdown anyway and had a newborn and a two-year-old, so even if we had been allowed to leave the house, doing so would have been a pipe dream anyway. We came home with the baby, and the next morning, my mother brought my older son home. He arrived with flowers from my mother's garden and his "Best Big Brother" shirt on. He sanitized his hands and came over to me on the couch and instantly looked at his brother in wonder. He asked to hold him and kissed his head unprompted. I looked at my two boys in that heart-warming moment and thought, shit, there are two of you.

YOU WILL MISS THIS

People love to tell young mothers that there will be so many things that they will miss as their children get older. I believe them because I am not so arrogant as to understand that people who came before me see everything in parenting hindsight. I believe they do have value to offer. However, just because you have experience with parenting, your experience is not necessarily my shared experience. Here are some things I absolutely do not (and will not) miss about having little ones.

Night feedings. I had someone at a hair salon tell me not to wish away night feedings because I would miss them. Do you know what has never happened once while getting to spend a night uninterrupted in my bed? I have never woken up and said to myself, "God, do you know what I really wish had happened last night? I wish I had been woken up by the piercing scream of my child at 3 AM only to frantically stumble through the dark and wrestle with those stupid snap pajamas to change a diaper, and then sit and feed them to return them to their crib and pray they go back to sleep until the sun was up." Never, ever have I said that.

All of the baby stuff consuming my house. I will not miss having to turn sideways to squeeze between my playpen and the couch just to get by. I will not miss stubbing my toe on the base of the baby swing. I will not miss baby bottles overflowing on my kitchen counter. I will not miss diaper genies frequently needing to be changed. I will not miss the gate that cuts my house in half. I hate stuff and I don't care how cute it is. I know I am done having babies because, as my youngest moves past a stage, and we can get rid of another item, I don't feel a sense of loss. I feel relieved. I didn't go crazy on my baby registry because I realized how short-lived all those items are used for. I'm glad I got the basics of what I needed. As much as a Bluetooth-enabled baby swing sounds fantastic, I didn't need a nap pod in the middle of my living room.

Diaper bags. Leaving the house is a marathon with babies. (One nice thing I will say about the pandemic was there were a lot less of those frantic dashes out the door). I will not miss doing such mental inventory: "Do I have enough diapers? Are there wipes? Do we have a change of clothes that will fit him in the inevitable event that he will puke or shit himself? Do we have a bottle packed? Where is the bottle warmer?" As my son has gotten older, we just basically throw a snack, water bottle and a clean pair of underwear in his bag just in case and we bolt.

Diapers. Buying them. Changing them. Feeling like a horrible human being for using disposable ones. Just ... diapers.

Carrying them everywhere. My back and shoulders have hit their brink. Yes, when they first start walking, that is a different kind of stress, but once they find their solid footing and don't try to put everything in their mouth, you can actually sit down (sometimes).

The mess from eating. One of my babies was spoon-fed; the other did baby-led weaning (more to come on that). They both made a mess. Baby-led weaning is one thousand times worse. At one point, we had a gross drop cloth under his highchair, and no matter how many times we washed it, it needed to be burned. It was disgusting.

Tantrums. I once comforted my son for over

an hour because he was inconsolable after the flowers in his imaginary garden died. I start tantrums as Florence Nightingale, but I go full on Nurse Ratched if it lasts longer than ten minutes. They.are.the.worst.

I look forward to the point when I don't have everything in my house rearranged constantly (for example, picking up tampons off my bathroom floor four times in one day). Picking up the same stuff repeatedly, every single day, is a monotony that I will not miss. If returning your couch cushions back to the couch from the floor 2,385 times a day is enjoyable, then parenting is for you!

Being interrupted constantly. On the phone. While trying to do something. While talking to my husband. I look forward to the day when I can have a conversation without having three others simultaneously happening on the side.

Having an audience while going to the bathroom, or in the odd event that they are not in the room with me, having someone banging and crying on the other side of the door because I had to use the washroom.

Car seats. I won't miss strapping a screaming infant into one, then a toddler. I will not miss carrying around the awkward, clunky infant car seat. I will not miss not being able to drive others around because my back seat is consumed by car seats. I won't miss cleaning them, installing them or adjusting them. Nor will I miss navigating their straps during the miserable Canadian winter. Bye!

Doing a stupid amount of mental math to figure out when I can shower, and then informing my husband of the fact that our shared responsibility of keeping our children alive will transition from a dual effort to falling on his shoulders for the next fifteen minutes, so I can go perform basic hygiene.

Taking care of little ones while you yourself are sick. If you are a parent, you know exactly what I'm talking about.

I will miss their chubby cheeks and their adorable little hands reaching up to be picked up. I will miss the excitement of watching them learn to walk and say new words, especially when my little one holds out his hands and says "peas" instead of "please." They will continue to learn, though, and I hope I continue to be amazed by that (I'm talking about learning coding, not how to use a vape). I will miss being their instant comfort zone— the minute I pick them up and I feel their bodies relax in safety. But I won't miss them needing me all the time. I will miss them grabbing a book, crawling into my lap and asking to read with them. Nonetheless, I will not miss everything. Stop telling us that we will. And stop assuming that helps us survive those depleting early years. It doesn't. Some of it just sucks, and our only requirement is to survive it. End of story.

WHAT IS A
WEEK-END?

Weekends with young children are not really weekends. Sure, you might not have to go into a formal job, but your second, more draining job is still there for you.

If you are a stay-at-home parent, I imagine your days just all blur together. Instead of the mythical promised land of rest where everyone around you just spurts out and leaves work on Friday, a weekend with young children feels more like a marathon in the Colosseum to clean up the disaster of the previous week and prepare for the next one.

There is no catching up on sleep, no Saturday to get your life together by cleaning, doing laundry, getting groceries, and then having a Sunday to sit on the couch and do nothing. My husband and I had our pre-kid weekends down to a routine. Saturday was our catch-up-on-life day to do the aforementioned activities and prepare for the week ahead. On Sundays, we did nothing. We slept in, ate a late breakfast, went out if it was nice or binged watched television if it was miserable out. Now, mini-series are my jam because it only takes me two months to watch those four-part series. I miss doing nothing with every fiber of my being because, with young kids, there is always something. I will not miss having to coordinate a weekend away months in advance to make sure there are no activities or events and to secure babysitting.

Wrestling to get them ready to go to the park that they don't want to go to is particularly fun. Pretending to be excited when you watch them go down the slide for the 534th time, then wrangling with them to go home from the park that they didn't want to come to 90 minutes earlier is not my favourite pastime.

I miss feeling rested and recharged going back into work on Monday. I miss Saturday afternoon naps because no one needs to be fed, played with, put down for a nap, worked through a tantrum or diaper changed. The entire thing is so mind-numbing that I want to go full Oedipus Rex on my own eyeballs. I really, really miss *nothing*.

PARENTAL LEAVE

There were a few key differences between my leaves. My first maternity leave was 12 months. I went back a week after my son had his first birthday. The second time, I went back to work after an 18-month maternity leave when my son was 17 months old. The intent the second time was to also return to work after 12 months, but with the dumpster fire that was 2020 and 2021 combined, I was going to stay out of the classroom for as long as I could possibly afford it before having to move back in with my parents.

You generally all know how the first maternity leave went. I had so much hope for the second, which obviously got crushed by Covid and the idiots who didn't think Covid is a thing because it inconvenienced their small lives. (Too harsh? I'm going to leave it). Even though the entirety of my second parental leave was bookended by the very beginning of the pandemic, I have to say it was still a better leave. Don't get me wrong, it sucked, but it was better than my first. I attribute that to two distinct things. The first is the fact that I was able to take an 18-month maternity leave. Babies at 12 months are still babies, despite formally moving into the designation of toddler. Most of them can't walk yet, as the average for that is 14 months (I don't know where this thing came from that babies are supposed to walk by their first birthday). They are also still teething and most of them still have to go from a two-to-one nap transition. A period of momentous change and shift happens for a child between the ages of 12 and 18 months. When I went back to work the first time when my oldest was one, I had no idea what I was in for. We still had a lot of rough nights because he was still getting so many teeth, including his one-year molars. He was in so much pain that he would often hit himself in the head with his hand or hit his head on the wall. I used to worry about that. Someone thought that he was doing that because he was vaccinated (we're not friends). As soon as his molars were out, he never once again hit his own head, but on the nights his molars were coming out, oh.my.god. There were times when I was awake with him at 4 AM, because when he started to transition to light sleep, he was more aware of his teeth, and by then, the copious number of drugs that I had given him had already worn off. There were multiple mornings when I went into work and cried at my desk because I just didn't know how I was going to function that day. My tears were wiped and compartmentalized before my students walked in because: (a) my teenage students wouldn't have understood, and; (b) my school would have only worried that I left supply plans had I not been able to function. The point is that by the time my second son was 17 months, my experience of going back to work was entirely different. He had already made it through all his nap transitions, which I was able to do with him at home, so he wasn't going through them at daycare and coming home a miserable crab. He was also walking and therefore more independent. He was able to start verbalizing some of the things he wanted to say, making it easier for him with his caregivers. I know that in Europe, depending on the country, some women can have as many as two years of maternity leave, and while I would love all the supports that a lot of European women get postpartum (hello, Scandinavian countries), I don't know that I would want a full two years off work. It's just not for me. Firstly, I like money. I like having money to buy food and keep my home warm. I also like money to pay someone to shape my eyebrows. Secondly, I like that my children were cared for by other people. This obviously did not happen to the extent that I wanted with my oldest, since he was pulled from pre-school, but he did still go to a home daycare, and my youngest was left with his grandparents for my first year back to work. Those extra months of grace were monumental in allowing me to be in a better place when I returned to work, and even though I was navigating teaching in a pandemic, it was more manageable than going back to a normal school year. That is saying a lot.

The other major difference between my two maternity leaves was my husband's parental leave. My husband's company gives him two weeks of paternity leave. That is somewhere in the middle in terms of progressive. There are some companies that I know of that allow spouses to take up to four months of paid parental leave, and their company will top them up to their full salary. My school board gives partners four days of parental leave, and one of those days includes the birth of the baby. Pathetic, isn't it? They claim to care for their staff and students, but really, it's just the latter. I could tell you horror stories of the way that some staff were treated during illness or while caring for a very ill loved one. You wouldn't be impressed.

Anyway, two weeks. That's what my husband got the first time. The first week he took off after our son was born, then went back to work for a week, and then took the second week directly after I ended up in the hospital and was basically comatose for five days with infection. In my first leave, all four of our parents were also still working full-time, which meant that I spent a lot of time alone with that child. I think a lot of our mothers' and grandmothers' generations don't get how we struggle so much now. Sure, babies haven't changed but motherhood has. A lot of our mothers had their own parents who were retired when they had children, and so they had more help. I think working part-time also truly used to be more part-time. There also weren't ridiculous expectations presented on social media, doctor's offices, horrifying mom groups online or the raving competition that is school (I will unleash on that later).

The government of Canada passed legislation the year in between my sons, which allowed for spouses to take up to five weeks of paid paternity leave. My husband was allowed to add this to his two weeks of paid paternity leave from his employer. That means that for almost two months, my husband was off with me. That was the difference. I wasn't alone at the beginning with a ruptured body that could barely get out of bed, having to provide milk, fresh from the cow, for the little one while the bigger one shit on the floor. My body had a chance to recover the second time. I was very much on notice for the first two weeks postpartum with my second. I treated those first 14 days like a countdown to another potential infection. I just waited for it, but it never came. When I got to the 21-day mark, I figured I was in the clear. This is also coming from someone who had a vaginal birth. For women who have cesareans, they can't drive for the first two weeks or lift their child's car seat or carry them. How on earth are they supposed to do that without 24/7 support? I healed properly the second time. There were no infections, no setbacks. I was able to successfully pump because there was always another set of hands available for those first six weeks. The birth of my son also occurred 13 days into the first lockdown in my province. I am well-aware that the only thing that kept me sane in that period was the fact that my husband was home. We were spun into an isolated cocoon, but even though we could not go anywhere or do anything, I was okay because I wasn't doing it alone.

Our society is so consumed by babies. Their beautifully appointed nurseries and their little hipster outfits, but we completely forget that a mother was also forged in fire. I just sweated for nine months and then continued to sweat for weeks after giving birth (you just wake up soaked like you entered a wet T-shirt contest in hell). Yes, babies need to be fed and cared for after they are born, but so do their mothers. A woman's entire world is shattered overnight when she becomes a mother. I don't care how blissful anyone says it is. Good or bad, the world you knew no longer exists. While mothers are often caring for their babies after birth, it is imperative that there is someone to care for the mother. I'm not talking about family that drops by with food but lingers to the point that you begin to glare at them because all you want to do is change your own diaper and take a nap. Whoever the mother's support person is, be it a spouse, sibling, friend or relative, that person needs to be accessible to that mother. She will leak at any point in 24 hours. She will be unable to get up off the couch because her postpartum contractions are so painful that it is taking all the energy within her not to scream. Her hormones will cause her to cry and rage in cycles for months. That is why parental leave provided by employers and governments is critical. Society wants healthier moms and babies? You make sure you give their support person the resources that allow them to be there. It is as simple as that—having a physical presence that is there to hold that mother's hand. The baby's just fine.

YOU CAN'T SAY THAT

*Disclaimer: I had two women, who experienced
infertility and infant loss, pre-read this chapter
before publication. As I did not experience either
of those things myself, I wanted to be sure that
I wasn't inadvertently being dismissive of those
experiences. They both encouraged me to publish it.*

Can we please stop assuming that all women six

months after their wedding or "of a certain age" want to discuss plans for their uterus with you? The questions that I got constantly shortly after my wedding were just extremely annoying to me, but to someone else, they may be completely devastating. So, can we please stop asking:

1. Are you pregnant?
2. Are you trying to get pregnant?
3. How long have you been trying for?
4. Have you tried (xyz)?
5. Do you want children?
6. How many do you want?
7. Do you think Nicole is pregnant? (This was not a question that was directly addressed to my face but one I overheard after a visit to our local steakhouse, and I was clearly full and bloated. I have no regrets).

I am done having children.

Think about that statement for a minute. For me, firstly, that statement is one of privilege. I wanted two children and was lucky enough to conceive them naturally. Secondly, I have access to birth control, which prevents me from a third unwanted endearment. I am aware of how lucky I am in both of those circumstances. We are also not trying for a girl because children are not collectibles. You don't need to have them all.

To some people, that statement might be more traumatic. For some, they might be done having children after one because that's all they wanted. For others, there may be PTSD that they are still processing from their first birth. For others, perhaps there was a medical issue that made having a second child impossible. For some, maybe they tried constantly to have another, and it just never happened.

My husband and I did not struggle with infertility. I have no concept of what it is like to have my eggs retrieved or to have to inject myself with hormones. I do not know what it is like to have my husband's sperm put into me in an office with an inseminator. My husband has no idea what it is like to have to ejaculate in a cup and race it over to the fertility clinic while it is still warm. I don't know what it is like to constantly have 6 AM blood draws or vaginal ultrasounds every day for two weeks. I can't imagine going through all of that with so much hope only to have the clinician come into the office and say, "I'm sorry." That's a hope that kills, I imagine. I did not experience any miscarriages or stillbirths, so I can sympathize with those stories, but I would never be ignorant enough to claim that I can empathize with them, because I can't.

I was consumed by loneliness with my first son,

even though I was never alone, and I imagine when you lose a baby, there is a loneliness in there that swallows you. You weren't alone there for those moments you had another human inside of you, however long or short. I imagine many women have the default setting of self-blame, even though the rational parts of our brain know there was nothing that could have been done differently. I know someone who lost their baby during the pandemic, and they were told it was because they got vaccinated. You must be a special brand of ignorant to think that is okay to say that to someone who just lost their child. I don't know the fear of finally seeing that positive line on the test after a miscarriage. For me, the longest moment of my life was waiting for my son to cry while the doctor removed the cord from around his neck. I do remember the agony of waiting for nine months to wait and see if your baby is going to make it while you carry the constant fear that you will lose them. I don't know what that feels like after having already suffered one loss. That you will be alone in and of yourself again.

You know what, though? Even though I don't know what such experiences feel like, I want women to talk about them to me. And I want to actively restrain myself from the cliche responses. What I want to do is learn how to listen. Mom guilt is a ravenous monster, and she goes for blood even during pregnancy. If a baby is lost, you likely have mom guilt because you are a mother even without that baby. Guilt is the twin of shame. We don't talk about these things because we are ashamed of them. Why is that? Why be ashamed about it? Let parents fill the space that they need. If they don't want to talk about it, that's fine, but if they do, they have a right to occupy that space. Think about our grandmothers and mothers and how alone they may have felt in those moments of motherhood. How many of them were hidden away when they struggled? I don't want that for my own version of motherhood, and I don't want my sons growing up thinking that is how a mother should be. I let my boys see me cry. Witnessing those moments of weakness will make them better men. I want my sons to understand that being a parent will be one facet of their lives, if they so choose to be, but I don't want them to be consumed by it.

If someone *wants* to share their experience of infertility with you, let them. Let them talk about it in whatever way they want. If there were negative moments or some positive ones, they are entitled to have all those moments. I told a friend prior to my second pregnancy that we had been trying for a few months to get pregnant, and it wasn't working. I was severely worried that something was wrong because I feared that the infection I had after my first pregnancy had caused some type of scar tissue or potential damage to my ovaries, fallopian tubes or uterus and was prohibiting a potential pregnancy. My friend told me about a specific type of cough syrup that the woman is supposed to ingest during her fertile period, which makes for an optimal environment for sperm. I'm not going to list the type here because I'm not a doctor and don't feel like being sued. I felt like I had nothing to lose by trying it, so I did. I got pregnant that month. Maybe it was the cough syrup, maybe it was just sheer coincidence and had nothing to do with it. I was okay with being vulnerable at that moment. Some other people might not be, and it is not up to you to make that decision of exposure for them. If someone is willing to share with you, though, I beg you, please remember that what you say in response that you think is helping probably isn't.

Here are some of the worst things to say:

1. Everything happens for a reason
2. It will happen when you just relax
3. It will happen when you least expect it
4. It all works out in the end
5. God has a plan for everything
6. The universe doesn't send you more than you can handle
7. Maybe you weren't ready for a child

I was the recipient of such phrases when I was dealing with my depression after my first pregnancy. It was infuriating. I imagine to a woman struggling with infertility that it is pulverizing. Honestly, do you really think there is a God sitting up in the clouds whose entire job is to decide who gets a baby? If that deity does exist, they absolutely suck at their job. I have seen multiple examples in my own life of people who would be great parents that struggled to become that. Some ended up becoming parents, some never did. Through teaching, I can assure you I have seen numerous instances of people who are completely undeserving and incapable of parenting. That entire department needs to be fired.

I remember when I worked on my first book and I explained to someone what it was about, she paused and said, "so, you're just complaining about your son for one hundred pages?" She believes that all children are blessings, and that motherhood is the ultimate fulfilment that a woman can experience in life. I hope you know where I'm going with this. I know some of you are thinking, "how dare she attempt to discuss infertility while she was privileged to have her two children without difficulty?" I imagine infertility is hard and demoralizing. I know motherhood is hard and demoralizing. This dichotomy of female suffering in the Colosseum of life to see who can claim ultimate martyrdom is relentless and insufferable. It needs to stop. A woman who is attempting to get pregnant is not entitled to get mad at me for saying motherhood is hard, and I have no right to tell a woman trying to get pregnant to just enjoy getting to take care of herself. I can pass another childless couple on the street and be envious of their freedom, lack of responsibility and independence. That same couple can watch me sweat while wrestling my feral child into his stroller and wish they were doing the same. I respect women who struggled with infertility but can still be real about the struggles of motherhood afterwards. You also don't have to feel like every moment with that child is a blessing because you tried so hard to have them. It's okay to not love every single minute, and there doesn't need to be guilt attached to that. Honestly, if you did feel that way, I may be tempted to claw at your skin to make sure you were not a Stepford robot.

The reality I ponder the most about is women who regret motherhood. Let's not pretend they don't exist. I don't believe that, in the end, I will regret having my children. I would be lying, though, if I said I don't regret the absence of certain things I want to do in life that having children made more difficult for me to do. For example, the thought of packing in my teaching career to pursue a dream of writing the next great thriller is unrealistic. When you have other beings whose sole concept of stability comes from you, my dreams are temporarily on pause. Some women do dive off the deep end to pursue their dreams, and I applaud them. Some come from nothing and build empires. Others have a spouse who makes a sizable income, which makes the consistent flit in and out of different careers possible. I love my children in a way that I didn't know love was possible, and simultaneously, I regret the loss of who I was before them. Those two things can co-exist. I have nothing but sympathy for a parent who feels regret as their main interaction with parenthood. I doubt anyone carries more guilt than that parent. Yet, most of them are likely still parenting.

Regret is a part of life, and we can regret relationships, friendships, careers, so I don't understand why there is this overarching assumption that people can't regret parenthood. You can't break up with your children; you can't send them back. It is the only decision in life that is irrevocable. I think that you can regret motherhood and still be a good parent, because even though you regret it, you are still here. That counts for something. To anyone reading this who feels that way, it is okay to feel that way. It's also okay to have days that you primarily regret amidst the days where you can't see your life any other way. You are not a bad person. You are just as much a flawed human being as I am. Neither one of us is better nor worse than the other.

It's okay to miss who you were before they were born. I wanted to leave my kid at the park an hour before I sat down to write this. Motherhood is hard. Wanting to be a mom (or not, as women can choose that, too), the process of becoming a mom and then surviving the decades of motherhood afterwards are all colossal shifts in someone's life with no precedent to hold on to. This shit is hard, and we don't have a right to tell someone else that they should or shouldn't feel a certain way with wherever they are in that process.

JUST EAT

There is a lot of stuff that I hate about parenting. In fact, I probably hate a solid 85% of it, but if there is one thing that is in my top three of hated things, it is feeding my children. Aversion, abhorrence, hostility, scorn—use whatever word you want. I loathe feeding my children.

Something happened at the hospital for my second son that did not happen the first time. The nurse was looking over my intake forms and after going through the standard name, address and necessary information, she asked me if I was planning on breastfeeding or formula feeding. I paused right away when she asked because no one asked me that the first time. I was denied formula the first time. I responded that I was going to try breastfeeding again but was open to moving to formula right away if necessary. After my first experience with breastfeeding, my husband was wary of me trying again. He ultimately supported me in whichever choice I made, but I think he was trying to spare me some agony. Remember the nurse and lactation consultant that I mentioned who ultimately told me it was time to be done with breastfeeding? She worked at the same hospital where I delivered. She was kind enough to do a house call for me because she is my mom's best friend. After a few months had passed, she contacted me and gave me the name of the head of the maternity board at the hospital. She asked me to write to her and explain what my experience had been at the hospital because she was appalled by my first experience. So, I did. I was skeptical of doing so at first, both because I didn't want to seem ungrateful and because I didn't really think it would make a difference. The letter was the inspiration for the breastfeeding chapter in my first book. She wrote me back, which I was not expecting, and apologized profusely for my experience and said that she would take what I had said to heart. I didn't think anything of it at the time, deleted the email and went about my day. It wasn't until my second delivery when I was asked prior to giving birth what my feeding plans were that I realized maybe someone had listened.

Breastfeeding with my second generally went along the same lines as my first. However, when I asked for formula for him in the middle of the night this time, it was given to me without hesitation or question. After a few days, I decided I was going to try pumping again exclusively. At one point, I started to feel the feverous lump developing in my chest again and right away recognized it as the start of mastitis. I saw a lactation consultant again at the 48-hour appointment. This time, I went in with my war paint on. I wasn't the new kid on the block anymore. Turns out, I didn't need it. The lactation consultant was young, probably younger than me. She answered a few questions I had, and when I asked her what I needed to do when I was ready to stop breastfeeding, she didn't flinch, recoil or shame me. She explained to me that I could safely stop by cutting out one pump every three days in order to dwindle my milk supply. Finally, someone just answered my question without making me feel guilty about it. I explained to her that I could feel the beginnings of mastitis developing, and she massaged the lump out. I want you to take your knuckles and then forcefully grind them into a bruise. Do this repeatedly for five to six minutes. That's what it feels like to get a calcified lump of milk to disintegrate in order to avoid an infection in my breast tissue like I had the first time. She told me that I had to continue to massage myself for the next two to three days in order to avoid a new lump forming. How you do this at home is by getting a bowl of warm water and putting it on your counter. You then take your bra off and take your extremely swollen, sore breast and place it into the bowl of warm water. While it is soaking in there, you take both hands and knead your breast as though you are making quarantine sourdough and cry because of how much it hurts. I remember looking at myself in the mirror while I was doing this with tears running down my face. I was crying so much from the pain that I also had snot running down my lips. I begged my body to cooperate and work through the calcifications in order to prevent another full-blown mastitis infection. I wouldn't have survived that a second time. Physically, yes, but I knew what that was going to do to me mentally, and I was terrified of returning to that bad place, so I kneaded for dear life. I dried myself off and carefully put my nursing bra back on. A few hours later, my entire chest was covered in bruises. I had to go through the same process and knead directly over the same bruised parts of my chest again later that day.

After a few days, the lumps didn't return, and I was mercifully in the clear from a mastitis infection. When I would change my clothes (sporadically, of course) in the first few days after my second delivery, I purposefully turned my back to the mirror because I didn't want to look at myself. When I eventually forced myself to do it, I was appalled at the offensive purple bruising all over my chest and my swollen stomach, legs and feet that were still retaining my pregnancy fluid. I remember sighing and generally saying, "screw it, you're not sick right now. Bruises will heal." They did.

Ultimately, exclusive pumping worked for six weeks. I refused to pump during the night. I pumped four times during the day. I would wake up in extreme pain, though, because of this. Imagine waking up with the weight of a cylinder block firmly across your chest combined with skin that is so stretched out (as you might experience when you get new, tight skin after a burn). I adamantly refused to give up sleep this time to pump, and it was working out okay. The only other reason I was able to pump was because my husband had his paternity leave. So, while I was pumping for 20 to 30 minutes, he had the boys occupied. My older son thought the pump was the greatest thing ever. He would take the hoses while lifting his shirt and haphazardly put the hoses next to his little nipples and say that he was making milk for his brother. He's sweet but may fail high school biology.

At the four-week mark, I knew my husband was going to go back to work and that pumping all day with a baby and two-year-old in tow was completely unrealistic, so I began to wean myself from pumping. I had enough milk in the freezer so that my son had breast milk exclusively for the first two months of his life. When I was weaned from the pump, which just sounded like a dying donkey by that point, my husband did one final wash and sterilization of the pump and repacked it back into its travel case. This time, I had been in control of my breastfeeding. I stopped not because I was sick or felt violated, but because I actively wanted to, and the only way to describe it after my first experience was redemption. I proved to myself that I could pump but didn't want to anymore, and both of those feelings are valid.

I admit that I inadvertently used my kids for an experiment when it came to feeding. With my first son, he was traditionally spoon-fed. There is a recent sentiment that holds that baby-led weaning is about to become the new "breast is best" slogan in that, if you don't do it, you are wrong and irrevocably damaging your children. I think of the trauma that phrase caused for me when I was trying to breastfeed the first time. I played this phrase obsessively over and over in my head, that I had to breastfeed, or I was hurting my son. I don't think forcing baby-led weaning on anyone is going to be productive either. Choose what works for your family, right?

With my first son I started with baby cereals and purees because I did what I knew at the time with the knowledge I had available to me at the moment. I knew what baby-led weaning was, but because I was fighting bigger demons at the time, I needed something that was safe and familiar, and so, I fed my son in the traditional way. Do I regret doing so at times? Yes, but do I allow myself a moment of grace and self-compassion for where my head was at the time? I'm working on it. I made the mistake of spoon-feeding for far too long. Breaking that habit was difficult, but we eventually did. With my second son, I went directly to baby-led weaning. When I gave him yogurt, he was given a spoon and generally had to figure it out. This was a disaster. I hated baby-led weaning at the start. We had a disgusting, old paint splash mat under my son's highchair that just began to smell after the food splatter. There were splotches of yogurt all over the walls, and 75% of his plate caked itself onto the floor. Multiple times a day, I was on my knees, picking up food off the floor. And later, like a heathen, he would return to eat the scraps off the floor that I missed.

The part I struggled with the most was the amount of food waste. We obviously didn't put an adult portion of spaghetti (the WORST) out in front of him, but it didn't matter what it was—a lot of it went to waste. I wrestled with this a lot, because I come from a family where you just don't waste food. I ultimately decided to stick with baby-led weaning. Eventually, he figured out how to use his pincher. (Do it: the motion of bringing your index finger and thumb together to pinch seems insignificant to us as adults, but to a baby, you might as well be asking them to diffuse a bomb). When he could start grabbing things and figuring out where his mouth was (it's on your face, how hard is that?), he was shooting a solid 60% from the free throw line, and less food was ending up on the floor. Since he was exposed to touching various textures right away, he is a better eater. He will not eat eggs for the life of him, but he is more willing to try different things we put in front of him. Even if he doesn't like something, he will swish it around his mouth and spit it out. He will do this a few times. My older son eats exactly two fruits: banana and passion fruit (it costs $2 per passion fruit, so you best believe he is eating every damn seed). He will not touch an apple or orange, but apple sauce is cool. If I could feed my older son a waffle with peanut butter on it at every meal, I would. I also remind myself that there is a kid's menu at restaurants for a reason. My mom reminds me constantly that I was a very picky eater growing up. But now, I will walk into any restaurant and would be open to eating anything on the menu. The only thing that I have tried that I will never in my life touch again is eel. I ordered it by accident once in Europe when I misunderstood the menu. I thought, whatever, I'll try it. Nope. Never again. I felt like I was eating Flotsam and Jetsam.

The main thing I loathe about feeding my kids is just the general fact that I have to do it. Prior to kids, if my husband and I didn't want to eat dinner, we would have a bowl of cereal or some toast. It didn't matter. When I went out with my older son as a baby, we could go out for lunch or meet up with some friends at the park and have picnics. During the pandemic, mealtimes almost became a breaking point. I would have to come up with something to make three times a day and deal with a baby that just threw most of it on the floor and a toddler that lost his shit because I put a potato on his plate (he still won't eat those, but fries are fine). On top of that, I had to clean up those messes three times a day. I was constantly one meal away from a breakdown. We don't make separate meals for everyone in my family. We make one meal, and it gets chucked onto a plate and put down in front of my kids. They can eat or not, but if they don't, then they can be hungry until their next meal or afternoon snack. Cruella, right? I am a snack totalitarian in that they have breakfast, lunch, an afternoon snack and then dinner. I refuse to be the mom who is asked for snacks all day long, the mom who carries Goldfish in my purse or the mom who cuts my son's sandwiches into adorable stars or his watermelon (which he won't fricken eat anyway) into little hearts. If you are that mom, I truly don't know how you haven't gone full *Shining* on your family. I tried to put cute little panda bear/animal toothpicks into his meal once to which he abruptly informed me that animals do not belong in food, and he promptly removed them. So, that was it. There were no more gimmicks. Food went in front of them. They chose to eat or not eat, and that was the end of the meal. Look, if you are making those adorable meals for your kid because doing so is a stress reliever or brings you genuine joy, then keep doing it. Truthfully, I wish I could find that instinct that makes me want to do that, but I just can't. If you're doing it, though, because of some unwritten societal obligation or because it makes you feel like a better mom than everyone else at after-school pick up, you need to ask yourself why that is a thing. Your child's teacher doesn't look at their flax, almond butter, star-cutout sandwich, heart-shaped organic cheese and unicorn strawberries and think, "yes, this child will win a Nobel Prize." They probably think your kid is an entitled shit.

Also, are we seriously expected to have a menu planned out for our children to eat for a perfect meal rotation in a week? Am I to make sure that my sons have a perfect representation of all four food groups at each meal? If that is the case, I am failing miserably. There was one night when my kid ate a hot dog and a Timbit for dinner, and that was it. I don't know who these parents are that are feeding their children lentil soup and crostini for lunch, but seriously, good for you. I'm not. My kid is profusely offended if I put a bean on his plate and will move it to the table as if I'm asking him to move a dead mouse.

Do I wish for my son to outgrow his rage-inducing picky eating like I did? God, I fricken hope he will. Outgrowing such pickiness comes from constant exposure and putting things on his plate repeatedly whether he likes it or not. Sometimes, he just touches the food. Other times, he will lick it. And in moments of radiating hope, there are even times that he takes a bite. Sometimes, he loses his shit, takes it off his plate and puts it on the table next to him. I honestly don't know how my child is still alive, but if you have a kid who literally survives on air and bullshit like mine, just know he's somehow still here, and your kid will be, too.

DO YOU GET IT NOW?

I remember one day on my first maternity leave when my husband got home from work, and I had just gotten the baby to take a cat nap in his bassinet. My husband looked like he was about to reach in and take him out, so I quickly interfered. I told him that just because he was home now, that didn't mean he could undo all the work that I had done during the day. When he got home from work, he was my reinforcement; he wasn't here to stir things up. In small exchanges, such as that one, my husband always liked to reiterate to me how he wouldn't know what maternity leave was like. He would tell me he had no idea what that meant, and even though he watched me go through everything, it didn't automatically mean that he understood what I was going through.

Maternity leave is extremely lonely. You are constantly at the mercy of someone else's schedule. You don't leave the house very often, and when you do, it is for very short spurts of time. You spend your days in the same four outfits that you wear in constant rotation. You don't wash your hair. You have no one else to talk to, so Google Home becomes your best friend. Sound familiar? The pandemic allowed others who generally would have never experienced the level of loneliness that accompanies maternity leave to catch a glimpse of what it feels like. Yes, the pandemic was worse because, on a regular maternity leave, you could meet up with your wolf pack. That is a term brilliantly coined by Ali Wong in her stand-up special *Hard Knock Wife*. There, she talks about how, after having a baby, a mother formulates and knits together her own group of women that are going through the same experience (as mothers) and how group members cling to one another. There is no other circumstance in which you would likely have ever met or hung out with these women, but as mothers, we are all so desperate for adult inter-action, that you weather the storm of maternity leave together. During the pandemic, there was ob-viously no wolf pack, and so it was even more iso-lating. I missed going to the library with my son, but I also didn't miss having to constantly watch the clock to make sure I got in the car early enough so that he wouldn't fall asleep for ten minutes in the car, only to ruin his nap entirely, and there-fore shatter my sanity. I did miss taking my sons to swimming lessons, but I did not miss having to make sure I was strategically shaved and plucked just to take my kid in the water. I did also miss going to coffee shops, but my bank account knew I was going to be on an extended maternity leave, so she didn't mind at all. Yes, my bank account is fe-male because she runs the show.

There really is no effective way to describe the already overwhelming loneliness of a regular ma-ternity leave fused together with a pandemic. I think, like we all experienced, the best way to de-scribe it was just the monotony of it. Everyday felt like the day before, and we went to sleep, knowing that tomorrow wasn't going to be any different. I remember, at one point, thanking God for the sea-sons in Canada because watching the progression of the seasons at least reminded me that time was actually passing. I remember when the weather finally got warm, it was easier to spend time out-side with my sons, and I felt so elated that I may as well have been an upper East Side divorcee, having Oysters Rockefeller at the Plaza with a Maltese on my lap. Just getting to go to a park with the sun on my face felt like the jackpot.

I mourned my maternity leave profusely. The pandemic stole something from everyone. For some, it may have been a job, a home, a relationship, a graduation, their mental health, their physical health and so on; for others, their lives were lost. I am fully aware of my privilege during the pandemic. I was not working, and therefore could keep both of my sons home with me, and my husband also had a job where he was able to work remotely from home. We existed in our little incubator. There is a common saying during the pandemic that we are all in the same storm, but we are not all in the same boat. I was not floating at sea with a lifejacket, but I was also not on Jeff Bezos' yacht either. I was somewhere on a fishing boat that had a motor that worked most of the time. Even though I know that I was lucky to be in the position that I was in, I am still allowed to mourn the loss of my maternity leave, and I will never apologize for that. No, I didn't have to work, but work is work, and it will be there when I get back. The first two years of my son's life? I don't get to re-wind that. I never get to have that with him again. I had so many plans this time. I was going to take my older son to museums and water parks during the week because once he started school, I was not going to have the chance to do that with him anymore. We were going to go away in the winter because when I am working, I am not allowed to leave my job during the school year. I will never know what it was like to take my second baby to the library, water parks or play groups. Those memories don't exist. I am well-aware that once we move past this, there will be an opportunity to return to normalcy, but never for me to experience my son's babyhood again. Time is a non-renewable resource. His older brother has pictures all over the place. On planes, in Europe, at waterparks, having dinner with relatives. My second son's first year of life was formally documented from our couch. I know that he won't remember any of this. I know he won't care, but I am not having any more children. I never got my shot at redemption. I was robbed of it a second time, and I will never, under any circumstance, apologize for grieving it.

THE SINK CADDY

I don't spend a ton of money. I abhor makeup in general, so I don't buy it. It's not that I have a thing against makeup. I'm actually that creepy person at weddings that you might catch staring at you because I'm thinking, "that's bloody amazing! How did they do that?" I just can't be bothered with it and hate the way it makes my skin feel. I do like to get my nails done and my facials, but shopping in general is not my thing. If I feel like something is drabby or I need something new, I'll go to the store with the specific intent of finding that item and leaving. I rarely go shopping for the sake of going shopping. My husband is the opposite. If I gave him my blessing to wreak havoc through the mall with our joint credit card, he would have no problem hitting our limit. During the pandemic, my husband, like most people, was constantly online shopping out of boredom. I don't mean he was constantly buying things, but he was always on various websites looking at things for fun. At first, he was buying things for his office to work from home. A random assortment of cables or computer stands would come to our door, and since it was for his home office, I didn't really think anything of it because he needed it to do his job. When it was announced that golf courses were opening, my husband ordered a pocket towel for golf balls. If, like me, you don't know what that is, it is a small sac that is designed to fit into the front pocket of your pants. Then, while golfing, if your golf ball is dirty, you simply place it into said sac, and it burrows in there to be cleaned. As ball-washing stations were off limits during Covid, my husband felt this was a necessary purchase. My husband doesn't just order random little items so that we constantly have packages at our door. He is very conscious of trying to optimize orders to have as many things come in one box at one time, so I couldn't play the environment card. I just called him an idiot under my breath and moved on.

But then, there was the sink caddy.

The sink caddy is what my husband and I like to call our "peak pandemic moment" because it was so insanely pathetic that, had it happened in the state of normalcy, I think we would have gotten divorced. We had a little old plastic container in our sink that held our sponge and the brush we used to clean bottles. We had two things on the counter: our mason jar with dish soap and a small bowl to put our wedding rings in while we washed dishes. At some point in the pandemic, my older son accidently knocked the small bowl over and broke it. A metaphor for our lives then at its finest. The mason jar was starting to leave a ring on our counter, and the plastic holder that we had just kept sliding down. It eventually cracked. So, we just recycled the plastic parts that we could and left the sponge and brush in the sink like the basic people that we are.

Then, one day my husband discovered sink caddies online. There are dozens of different designs that are all created with the purpose of holding everything you need at your sink in one location. He ran up the stairs to show me some of his favourite designs. We spent an hour looking at different makes and models. Did we want chrome? What about black? Would white stain too easily? Then, there were other difficult choices. Did we want the caddy to be able to hold our mason jar of soap or were we going to leave this on the counter? Ultimately, we couldn't decide and chose to sleep on it. "We will decide tomorrow!" Decisions are better made in the morning. In the end, we decided to go with a chrome finish for our caddy that had a removable tray to collect water and thus protect our counters. It also has a separate compartment to hold our sponge and bottle brush, all while being ergonomic enough to hold our dish soap and the shot glass we now use for our rings. It was twenty dollars, but to us, we may as well have bought a new car. When we got the email saying the item had shipped, we checked frequently to see when it would arrive. When we heard a delivery truck on our street, our ears would perk up and we would run to the window to see if it was coming to our driveway. We eventually received confirmation that it was going to arrive on a Monday, so I checked the front porch repeatedly until it arrived. It was everything that I could have possibly hoped for. I took it out of the box, washed it, and then organized the disarray of contents around our sink into one unified, compartmentalized system. It was a thing of beauty. My husband came up from the basement where our office is and walked around the counter, looking at it. He removed the sponge and put it back in like the way you would check how the seat of a new car is adjusted. We were elated.

Looking back now, I think the sink caddy was a microcosm of our lives in that moment of the pandemic. It was always a mess. Things were disorganized. We were so desperate at this point that we used to argue about who went to pick up dinner because it meant we had ten minutes alone in a car. In one week that was particularly desperate we argued about who got to put out the garbage in -20 in January because it allowed us to just not be in the house with our children for five minutes (I won that argument by the way).

It truly didn't matter what we did to stay on top of the chaos, we just couldn't. It felt like we were drowning. When the sink caddy arrived, it allowed us to exert some control over the situation because we had nothing that could control the world around us yet (this happened before vaccines were available). Like I said, had the arrival of a sink caddy brought us that much glee pre-pandemic, I think it would have been a sign for us to go our separate ways. If that was the most significant thing in our marriage that we had to look forward to, I would have thrown in the towel. Now, it's just a funny story, and I mean, practical, as the caddy is still my best friend in the kitchen.

We were quite lonely, in the heat of cabin fever and so bored that the arrival of something so insignificant as a sink caddy made our entire year. Forget that our second son had also been born that year, the star of the show was definitely that sink caddy. If you think about it, you probably also have something just as ridiculous that will end up being your definitive "peak pandemic moment." Maybe it's pathetic, maybe it's heartbreaking, maybe it was productive, but hold on to that moment, so post-pandemic, you remember that you're not there anymore.

HYSTERICAL

Having a baby changes your body forever. I'm not talking about the way that it looks. I'm talking about the way it works, as in it doesn't. I had my first son when I was 29 years old. My second was born when I was 31. That may not seem like a big deal, but for me, jumping the threshold into my thirties between pregnancies was a monumental shift. If you are having your first baby in your thirties, you don't know any differently, but I had straddled the line for pregnancies, and I felt it.

My first pregnancy had all the standard pregnancy delights: stretch marks on my chest, some on my stomach but most on my thighs. Guess I forgot to put my fancy shea butter cream down there or I just couldn't see my thighs anymore and didn't particularly care. The second time, it was more of the same. There was a shift after the second pregnancy, though. Your body is older, it is more tired, and it feels it. I was well-aware that stuff was just broken and never going to work again. The warranty had expired. For example, my breasts now need a super supportive bra to keep them at a respectable height. Memory foam is required for holding them up like being palmed by the hands of angels. My stomach, no matter what I do to it (and honestly, I don't go out of my way here), will always have just that little hint of Jell-O across the top. My thighs are a lost cause, but they are great for holding a tray to eat ice cream off. I like the way they fill out my jeans now. The problem is no one wears jeans anymore apparently. I have learned exactly how to clamp my inner thighs together when I'm about to sneeze in order to minimize leakage. Yes, women leak after having babies. I also noticed that there was just a lot more pain in general. My back was sore, yes from pregnancy, but from carrying around a butter ball and a jealous toddler, too. My back was shot. I had shooting pain whenever I would get off the floor. The worst, though, was when I would have my periods. Oh. My. God.

I was very fortunate that prior to pregnancy my periods had always been relatively easy to handle. I had some back pain and light cramps for one day, but I never needed medication to get through them. That was not the case after pregnancy. Once my periods came back, I was a mess for 14 days out of a 28-day cycle. Think about that. That means that for half of every month, I was struggling with menstrual issues 13 to 14 times a year for potentially the next 20 years. Between my pregnancies, I just bore it. When I was ovulating, it felt like I was waking up with morning sickness all over again. I was nauseated for days, and sometimes, I threw up. Then, when my period started, I had cramps that felt like I was in labour all over again. There were times when I was teaching, and a cramp would hit. I would grip my desk and just clench my teeth until it passed. I don't know what my students thought was happening, but they were never brave enough to ask. It was unbearable. I needed a steady dose of Advil to get through the first three to four days of my period. When my son was finally asleep, I would build a strategic fort of pillows around me and place a warm bean bag across my abdomen. I would also lose so much blood that I would get severely lightheaded and feel extremely faint if I went too long without eating. Fainting couches were not designed for melodramatic women to collapse on gracefully in history. Such women were probably bleeding and hungry. Girl needed some cheese.

The only relief I had in my second pregnancy was not having to deal with periods for nine months. That was about it. Once my period came back after my second son, the same bullshit returned with a vengeance. At first, I talked to my family doctor who told me to just take Advil to get through it, as periods were just a part of life (thanks!). I am so tired of women being deemed as hysterical whenever they complain of reproductive pain. We are often dismissed and belittled and just told to suck it up because it is part of being a woman. I ended up talking to my OBGYN about it, and he suggested an IUD if I was done with having children. He took me a little bit more seriously. He said I was young and, with a gentle chuckle, asked if I was sure I was done. I laughed, he laughed again, and I called the pharmacy for the IUD in front of him. IUD insertion is not for the faint of heart. He told me that I likely wouldn't struggle with it too much because I had already had children, but for women who hadn't, they often claim it is the worst pain in their lives. I was just instructed to take Advil two hours before my appointment. I swallowed those pills, said a Hail Mary, walked into my doctor's office with my $400 IUD (insurance, praise be) and pre-pared for what I thought was going to be an im-palement. It wasn't horrible. But I mean, it wasn't great either. We weren't at Disneyland, but if a few minutes of pain meant that I wasn't dealing with unbearable periods every month, I was going to take it. My doctor talked me through the entire procedure and worked extremely quickly. He forced my uterus into a contraction (I didn't know you could do that) and told me when to breathe in and out. He showed me the IUD prior to insertion. It's hot pink because why would it be any other col-our? And then, with one slow exhale, he used what I can only describe as a miniature pogo stick with the IUD attached to it and plugged it up my vagina through my cervix (which was firmly shut this time) and lodged it neatly into my uterus. Once in-serted, he quickly removed the pogo stick and the forceps that kept my vaginal opening available to anyone who dare enter. I was sore for about a day after. Then, after insertion, I bled for around 20 days. After that, my next period was for 15 days, and from there, it would continually decrease. I barely bleed anymore. One to two days of spotting is it. I don't struggle with lightheadedness because I'm not draining iron as much every month. My cramps have also been tamed. That IUD was one of the best things to ever happen to me.

The most persistent issue I had that would not alleviate was my back pain. Eventually, it got to the point where I was having issues with vertigo, too, so I began to see a physiotherapist and chiropractor. This was my first time ever seeing a chiropractor, so I had to get X-rays done before he could begin to work on me. Feeling the little things and issues that lurk in your bones is one thing, but seeing the havoc that was unleashed on your body in black and white is another thing entirely.

While going over my X-rays, the doctor pointed out a few key things of concern. The first was my neck, which has no curve; it's just a solid straight line. That one, I can't blame on pregnancy. That's just because I like to sleep on my stomach and side. The two other areas of concern I can blame on my children. The first was two discs in my spine right at my bra line. Instead of having the necessary space between them, they were starting to overlap on one another like dysfunctional tectonic plates. I have boobs. They are heavy (no pun intended, I mean, they are literally heavy to carry around). During pregnancy, that heaviness became so unbearable to the point that my spine apparently started to wither under the weight. The fact that, after having a baby, you are hunched over them for months didn't help with how round my back had become. He was going to have to force them to separate. A breast reduction was put on the table as a viable option I'm considering.

The more disturbing realization came when, prior

to moving the X-ray slide, he asked me if I had painful periods. The look on my face must have clearly answered his question, and he proceeded to show me the X-ray of my pelvis. I saw my little IUD buddy on my X-ray, and she was pretty cute. Maybe I'll forgive the fact that she was hot pink as if automatically being that colour equates to female empowerment. You know those horrible period cramps that had made me feel like I was in labour? It's labour's fault. The doctor said that between carrying my pregnancies and then through giving birth, there was so much blunt force trauma to my pelvic bones that my left one, instead of being at a slight 45-degree angle as was normal, was almost at a 90-degree angle. My pelvic bone being so far out of proper alignment was forcing my uterus to be compressed because it didn't have the room it needed to just sit flopped over like it is supposed to. So, what was happening during my periods was that my uterus, when trying to contract to get rid of its lining, was pressing up against my pelvic bone, and that was causing the extremely painful cramps. My uterus was trying to do its job but had nowhere to go, so it had to bang up against my pelvic bone. I was just hysterical, though, right? Moral of the story: don't talk back to your mother. There were days when you broke her spirit, and I can assure you, you definitely broke parts of her body.

Ultimately, between the chiropractic care and physiotherapy, I was able to work on some corrections for my back. They didn't eliminate the pain entirely, but they made it a less-consuming issue in my day-to-day life. What didn't stop was the nausea with my periods because that comes from your ovaries. An IUD, unlike the birth control pill, does not stop you from ovulating. It stops you from building a uterine lining that is strong enough to sustain a pregnancy while also keeping sperm out. I imagine my little hot pink IUD, which I have named Lydia, stands guard at the bottom of my cervix with a lightsaber and slices through any rogue sperm dumb enough to try and get through (and sperm are pretty dumb. There are millions of them in a single shot, and only around 200 even make it through the uterus up to the fallopian tubes to fumble around and find the egg. So, I mean, their scoring percentage is not great). I was tired of feeling like I was getting early onset morning sickness once a month. I called my OBGYN again, and point blank asked him if a hysterectomy was something I could have. The short answer was no. He told me that because my issue was nausea, that was a hormonal issue that stemmed from my ovaries. In a hysterectomy where bleeding is the problem, I was informed that I could have the inside of my uterus cauterized or, to get any relief from my symptoms, I would have to take everything out, including my ovaries. He proceeded to tell me that for anyone under the age of 55, hysterectomies are only done if the issue is life-threatening. By removing the ovaries of a woman

that is still fertile (I hate that word), it drastically increases her chances of having a heart attack
and stroke. I remember saying, "I'm sorry, what?"
He repeated himself. I was in disbelief that those
two evils stepsisters were capable of wreaking that
much havoc on my body. Apparently, ovaries are a
Catch-22: I guess you can't live with them, but you
can't live without them either. This is what women
go through to have a baby, to not have a baby, to
try and control their periods, only to find out that
Mother Nature can be a real bitch, and the house
never loses. Women go through enough. Time to
step up to the plate, boys.

VASECTOMUS

My husband and I had agreed that, after the birth of our second son, he was going to get a vasectomy. I had already had a discussion with my doctor that in the case that I was going to need a cesarean with my second pregnancy that I wanted to get my tubes tied at the same time. I mean, I was already cut open, you might as well have at it. He told me that he could do that because I had discussed it ahead of time and made it very clear that was what I wanted. He said had I just blurted that out in the moment during my cesarean, he would not have honoured my request, as I likely would not have been in the right state of mind. I mean, yeah, probably. I didn't end up having a cesarean, and so, my fallopian tubes were open for business. That meant my husband's testicles needed to file for bankruptcy. He went through his family doctor and made the necessary arrangements to have one. At the appointment, he was asked once again if he was freely consenting to the procedure. Really? Did the doctor think he was going to look up and see me standing outside the window, dragging a finger across my throat to coerce my husband into having a scalpel slice through his scrotum? Because of Covid, it took a little bit longer to get an appointment, but luckily, my husband was on top of the process and had started it early enough that he was able to get it done when my second son was nine months old.

He was to have his procedure at a private clinic (still covered by insurance in case you are wondering), but there was a snowstorm the night before. I didn't care. We had made sure that he already had snow tires put on his car. Nothing was going to stop us from that appointment. I didn't care if it took us three hours to drive there when it should have only taken us forty minutes. I had done my part, and it was his time to shine. We woke up early that day and made sure his car was cleaned off and on we went. I wasn't allowed to go into the clinic with him, so instead, I had brought a bunch of blankets and hot tea with me and sat in the car. There were no malls open, and I couldn't just go into a coffee shop and hang out. Everything was in lockdown again. I waited in the car for almost two hours. I had downloaded a movie on my phone and just watched it, bundled up in the car. I was away from both of my kids for an entire morning when we were constantly at each other's throats at home, and even though I could have gotten frost-bite, it was glorious. My husband walked out in his jeans after the procedure, which was 15 minutes total, he said. I told him to wear sweats, but nope, he needed jeans that day, and I drove us home. We got sushi on the way home, and aside from the fact that my husband had to stay in bed for the rest of the afternoon with an icepack shoved in a jock-strap, it really was anti-climactic. Since I couldn't go into the room with him, I slipped a note into his pocket and told him to read it while he was waiting for the doctor:

Dearest Husband,

I'm sorry I'm not allowed in with you to stroke your head as though you are a Cheshire Cat as you tried to do for me while I was in labour the first time. You were smart enough the second time to just leave me alone entirely.

Just tell yourself as you undergo your 20-minute procedure, which you are allowed to be nervous for, that you are stronger than you know. If I could survive the simplicity of 79 weeks and three days of pregnancy, 56 weeks of morning sickness, 20 hours of labour, three stitches, 12 weeks of postpartum bleeding, being wheeled through the hospital with a fever of 41 degrees, with infections in my uterus and both breasts, with a two-week old baby at home, you, too, will find the strength to make it through.

*Remember, it's not a vasecto**my**, it's a vasectum**us**! Mask on, balls out.*

Love,
Wife

P.S. If you are in doubt, remember the sounds of screaming and tears throughout our house at 3 AM from both the babies and me.

My husband is fine and still a man, contrary to the belief of many insecure men-children. In fact, he is more of a man because he knew that his 20-minute procedure and 48 hours of rest were nothing in comparison to the destruction that my body went through; therefore, he took it upon himself to do what he could to alleviate all the responsibility and burden of birth control that had wreaked havoc on my mind and body for our first twelve years together. That's a partner. So, not only is my husband now shooting blanks, but I have the Iron Curtain up in there. If another baby ever gets through all of that, it's the second coming of Christ.

BEDTIME
BULLSHIT

Why is it that my child suddenly becomes severely dehydrated at bedtime after telling me that he was not hungry or thirsty all day? I used to think that putting a baby to bed was difficult. My husband and I had an entire routine down to a rhythm: we moved in unison; towels, creams and bottles were all placed out in strategic sequence, and; we had everything down to a perfect 27-minute Broadway performance. I used to think it was so much work putting a baby to bed until I had to put a three-year-old to bed.

My older son is now a great sleeper, and I completely acknowledge sleep-training for that. However, getting him into bed is an entirely different game. First, there is the song and dance about how he doesn't want to go to bed. Eventually, we get him up the stairs. Then, he tells me he doesn't have to pee. I am not changing sheets in the middle of the night, so scene two generally focuses on him just doing the simplest thing in the world but arguing about it with me for 10 minutes. Then, there is the toothbrush. I absolutely hate brushing my son's teeth. I don't know why it makes me so angry, but there is something about it that just feels so demeaning. First of all, when he sees floss, he acts like I'm going to somehow use it to give him a lobotomy. Eventually, I can floss his two front teeth, which are the only teeth that really require solid flossing because they actually touch each other. Then, I have to manage to get the toothbrush into his mouth. This generally involves biting and chewing on the brush for a moment, followed by another agonizing two minutes of "you are hurting me!" Now, of course, as the fully capable three-year-old that he is, he insists on brushing his own teeth. That's a disaster because I think he manages to only clean a solid eight of his twenty teeth. Then, there's rinsing, which generally just involves water ending up on him, the mirror, all over the counter—anywhere but the actual sink. I mean, do I really need to care that much about his baby teeth? Aren't they all just going to fall out anyway? Don't even get me started on bath night, and God forbid, I have to wash his hair. I make sure all the windows are closed those nights so that our neighbours don't think I'm waterboarding him.

When we finally manage to leave the godforsaken bathroom, there is a meltdown where he backs into the corner because I have the audacity to put soothing lavender lotion on him like the monster that I am. So, most times after a bath, I choose to lose that battle. I'm not going to hell over lavender lotion when I am within 30 minutes of freedom. He is now able to put his own pajamas on. They are usually inside out or backwards, but I do not care. Him putting on his own pajamas buys me a whole five minutes to wash my own face. Then, he needs to peruse his bookshelf with about as much fervor as a hipster, writing his screenplay at the local coffee shop all day. My blood pressure is usually borderline dangerous at this point. When he finally picks one of the same five books that he always picks, we can calmly snuggle and read the story. Then, anywhere from three to seven of his stuffed animals, Mufasa and his dinosaur all need to be tucked into bed. And they are tucked in with him in a strategic sequence so that Butter and Fernando do not bother one another but are close enough to Mufasa that he can protect them from a potential thunderstorm in the middle of January. Oh, and the dinosaur likes to have her own pillow. If you think my child sleeps in a king-size bed with all his little stuffed animals, you are wrong. He sleeps in a twin, and his stuffies consume more of the bed than his actual body. Then, comes the hardest part—getting to leave.

Since we sleep-trained my son as a baby, he has never needed us to fall asleep. We say goodnight to him, tuck him in and leave the room. I don't have to lay with him until he falls asleep. Where the actual rage kicks in happens in the doorway. Suddenly, when I try to leave the room, my son becomes Socrates. I say that not because Socrates was a great philosopher, but because his contemporary Greeks found him extremely annoying. Here are some of his greatest hits:

1. Why are Koalas fluffy?
2. What happens if the thunder reaches through my window and grabs my foot?
3. It's okay, Jesus will visit me. (I'm not sure how to handle that one).
4. Mommy, why do you love me?
5. Mommy, I want to put Scar in your bed to protect Dad just in case Dad has night-

mares.

6. Mommy, why is my penis small?
7. I will eat pizza when I am big.
8. What are those round, chubby things? (Points to my chest).
9. Mom, I love you because you take care of me. (After I have told him repeatedly to get back into bed).
10. You know what is so good? Jam, but only on waffles, not on eggs.
11. I like our eye doctor. She is cute.
12. Mom, how do you pee if you don't have a penis?
13. Looking at the Christ the Redeemer Statue on his wall atlas:

S: Who is that?
M: Christ the Redeemer in Brazil.
S: Who is Christ?
M: Jesus.
S: No, it's not, because he has his arms out like this. (Stands up in bed and mimics the statue).
M: Yes, Jesus stands like that a lot. What is the problem?
S: Jesus puts his hands like this. (Brings his arms in like a T-Rex).
M: That's baby Jesus. It is all the same person.
S: No, Jesus is just a baby, mom. That is a man.
M: Okay, buddy, it's not Jesus. It's just a man.
S: That's what I told you. You just needed to listen to me.
M: (Internally compresses rage).

When I manage to say the final good night, he becomes so consumed with thirst that he needs to get back out of bed to have his final sip of water, which accidentally manages to spill a little bit on his mouth somehow. Then, a towel is required to mop the egregious drop that has slid onto his chin.

Now, I am generally the one who must do this because my husband, God forbid, should be able to tuck him into bed. Only mom is allowed to send him to bed. That was never the case prior to the pandemic. If one of us was out, he simply was put to bed by whomever was home. When Covid hit, though, we were home all the time anyway and fell into a new rhythm where my husband put the baby to bed (ah, the "easy routine," which is now so easily done with one person. I roll my eyes at my past self for the production that was bedtime). Eventually, once my older son is in bed, I manage to drag myself to my room to put on my pajamas and am so spent from the encounter that I spend the rest of the night on my couch. There was onc night that was so rough that, in a final act of defiance, he got out of bed 20 minutes later when I was already taking a bath (stupid on my part—I flew too close to the sun again). He proceeded to walk right past my husband to storm the bathroom and inform me that he needed to use the bathroom. When I told him to just go, he insisted that he use the bathroom I was in because he wanted to spend time with me. He then got his toilet seat and stool from his own bathroom and dragged it into ours, so he could crap on the toilet all while I was in the bathtub. He proceeded to wipe himself, put his pajamas back on, wash his hands and then ask me to tuck him in. I got out of the bathtub angrily and quickly wrapped a towel around myself to walk him back to bed. He proceeded to cry while I did this because I was supposed to be wearing pajamas. That night was a new low.

Bedtime is so triggering for me. You are fully out of patience from every demand, tantrum, defiance and lack of appreciation that you have encountered during the day, and when you walk up those stairs to bedtime, you can smell your freedom. You are thirty minutes away from a glorious session of watching Netflix while eating everything from your secret stash of snacks that you refuse to share with your children. That's why when something so simple as crawling into bed becomes a full-blown riot, I crack. A lot of nights, I just lose my patience and give into small annoying requests ("Mom, my body is telling me it needs to do a somersault before bed") because in those moments, when liberation is within reach, I don't want to deal with another tantrum or meltdown, so I give in. I pick my battles during the day. But at bedtime, my reserves are depleted, so I kiss dinosaur, Mufasa, Butter, Fernando, Little John and whatever other annoying little creature he needs to sleep with, as well as him, so they can all have "good dreams." When all is said and done, I make sure that his blackout blinds and curtains are closed like a vault because, in my house, the sun rises and sets when I say it does. Does he hear the other children still playing outside in the summer? Sure. Do I care? Not one little bit. Just go the hell to sleep because I have to survive you all over again tomorrow.

The one thing I try to do every night with my son is ask him what his favourite part of our day was. I will say that mine was something simple, like how we made muffins, even though it absolutely was not, as our baking experience destroyed our kitchen and yielded a disastrous mess that had me wiping chocolate chips off the backsplash. As my son is three, he has no concept of time, and there-fore, one day, he will say he is so excited for next week when it's Christmas (this was said in July) or tomorrow, when we go to Europe together, he is going to try pizza. So, I mean, a little off topic, but eventually, he will zone in on something we did that day (whether it was going to the park, going for a walk, whatever). I do that just as much for him as for myself so that in the days when we have broken each other, when I have let my rage get the better of me, when he has hit me or his brother out of frustration, I want the last mem-ory in his head to be a good one, something that makes him happy. And I do this so that he knows that the entire day, no matter how hard, was not all bad. I also allow it as a moment to forgive myself. Yes, sometimes, the days are just horrible, and I want to press fast-forward or rewind, but in that moment when he tells me that colouring with me was the best part of his day, I remind myself that I am doing the best that I can in the only ways that I know how. That's all any of us can do, as well as hope that they don't live in our basements when they are thirty.

JEKYLL AND HYDE

Remember when I said that the newborn phase was hell? I was wrong. Well, not entirely. It is hell, but they also are super snuggly. I was ignorant to the realities of surviving toddlerhood. I also severely underestimated how often I would get hit in the face.

I get progressive discipline. I get speaking with validation, being on a child's level, helping them emotionally regulate and surviving their tantrums, not ending them, but holy shit. I had heard about the "terrible twos," the "threenagers" and the "F-you fours." All those terms are accurate. I choose to refer to my older son as Jekyll and Hyde. He can be the sweetest, kindest little boy in one moment, and thirty seconds later, turn into the monstrosity that is Hyde. It's hard to be calm and logical with a little being who, in a Hyde episode, is completely incapable of either. Some episodes force him into such a rampage that I have to walk away from him until I can come back and ultimately ask, "are you done?" Most of that is for my own self-regulation because if I don't physically remove myself for a break, I am worried I am going to punch him in the face. When he was a baby, sometimes, I would go to my bedroom to scream with the door shut after safely depositing him in his crib. When he was a toddler, I hid in my closet and rocked back and forth until the crying stopped (me, not him). Here are some examples of things that made my son mad in the trying third year of his life:

- Asking him to not "put his brother in the

garbage"

- Asking him to pee before leaving the house
- Asking him to put his shoes on
- Putting his shoes on the correct feet
- Asking him to take his shoes off
- Refusing to let him eat a cupcake before bed
- Receiving his plate from his Dad instead of me
- Breakfast on his orange plate, not blue
- Washing his pillow
- Tucking him in "incorrectly"
- Putting on his winter coat (-40 outside)
- Pouring his milk just shy of his cup's top rim
- Putting him down on a certain part of the floor
- Brushing his teeth
- Spreading peanut butter on his banana
- Attempting to put a new vegetable on his plate
- Giving him a brother
- Telling him he had to wear boots in the winter
- Telling him it was bath time
- Telling him it was time to get out of the bath
- Washing his hair (it's like an exorcism)
- Not letting him use the vacuum like a bat
- Santa not taking his brother away
- Hearing or seeing the waffles pop in the toaster (apparently, you can get offended by that)
- The sizes of pancakes we make
- Giving him a blue shirt instead of a pink one
- Sitting beside him
- Not watching two movies in a row
- Prohibiting him from carrying the mail key
- Asking him to carry the mail key

- Trying to give him a hug
- Cutting his toast diagonally instead of in half
- Me, breathing and existing

Like I said, I get progressive discipline, and maybe Jekyll can handle it, but Hyde sure as hell can't. You can't rationalize with the raging, morally ambiguous character that is Hyde. You need to just weather the metamorphosis until Jekyll comes back.

RAGE, BUT SELF-CARE

Here is a list of things that mothers with young children are told to be grateful for:

1. Getting to take a shower
2. Getting to sleep
3. Eating a meal that's warm
4. Time away from their children

These things are not privileges. They are necessities, and I absolutely will not profess my gratitude for having them. Hygiene is just a basic human requirement—how arrogant of me—much in the same way that sleeping and eating are. These make up the bottom of Maslow's pyramid as the most basic requirements that a human needs in order to function. Crying in the shower for a five-minute morning meditation is not self-care. Plus, the whole time you are in there, you are hearing phantom crying anyway, so it's not like there is an actual separation. Showers do get easier over time. When I had my first son, I could only shower if he was asleep or my husband was home. When he turned about two, I just made sure that the gate at the top of our staircase was closed and would yell out if he was okay every two minutes or so. I mean, he always responded, so no need to call Child and Family Services. He's fine.

I have never experienced rage in the way that I have as a mother. It is an ugly monster. It hatches in the pit of my stomach and slowly creeps up my spine before firmly implanting into my shoulders and flushing my face into an unrecognizable flare. There are days when I just blatantly don't like my children. I'm allowed to think that, and shockingly, I'm also allowed to say that out loud, and no, I'm not a bad mom. During particularly difficult tantrums, I have been headbutted (unintentionally), scratched and hit. I am disregarded daily and become a rote audio recording of requests that are so simple, and yet the requests are met with such mind-blowing resistance that I am depleted entirely. I have been screamed at and clung to within the span of 30 seconds. It is a thankless relationship of constantly giving with no reciprocation. If you think about the specifications that I just described in any context outside of a parent-and-child dynamic, I would be describing an abusive relationship. Motherhood, especially during the pandemic, brought out a Medusa in me that I didn't know how to control, as every day, I dragged my body out of bed for the remixed version of hell that yesterday had been. Having little children makes you a servant. You are required to provide for their every single need physically, mentally and emotionally. I felt like Cinderella, but no one was coming to save me. Except take-out. I will accept take-out over a prince every time.

The life altering responsibility of parenting comes with 24/7 expectations. If you are not a parent, you have no right to comment on any decision I make as a parent simply because you don't get it. I don't care what you think you know; if you are not a parent, you have no idea what I'm going through. *You just don't.* I'm not talking about turning a blind eye when a child is being abused, but it's not your place to comment on what my kid is eating or wearing. With my first son, his sleep was such a disaster at the beginning that when we had finally created a sleep eco-system that worked, we did everything to preserve it. Nothing was going to alter that sleep niche. We would miss events or have only one of us go. Alternatively, we would leave early or go without my son while he was left at home with a grandparent. People would comment to me about how my son never came to things, to which I promptly replied that I was the one who had to deal with him at 3 AM, so I was the one who decided his schedule. The best part is that those comments usually came from people who were not parents.

During the pandemic, fulfilling the expectations of motherhood became impossible. I could not be a good mother every day. And I wasn't. Their physical needs were met every single day in that they were fed, clothed and their sleep needs preserved, all at the expense of mine. In terms of meeting their emotional needs, some days, I did, and some days, I absolutely did not. I was so worried about my older son not being in daycare that I was online while he was in bed, trying to come up with activities for him to do. Sometimes, it would take me 45 minutes to set up an activity that would take him 15 minutes to complete. I didn't read to my second son anywhere as much as I did with my first because, with my first son, reading had been a coping mechanism that I instated to calm both him and I down while I was spiraling. I read to him a lot.

With my youngest, the luxury of that time evaporated. I now had to meet all the physical feeding and sleep needs of a baby while also meeting the needs of a two and then three-year-old. I can't even think of particular examples of what made the days so hard because they truly have all blended together into one relentless nightmare. Yes, there were moments of love, of course, but not enough to sustain me. I had become the sole outlet of every facet of society that my sons required. I was now their mother, their playmate, their coach, their chef, their maid, their preschool teacher. Being all those things had to be taken at the expense of something else, and that expense was my own existence. When my husband returned to work after his paternity leave, the full weight of the pandemic fell on me like that ton of bricks fell on Cersi during *Game of Thrones*, except somehow, I wasn't dead. The weight just collapsed on me the minute my feet hit the floor in the morning, and I spent the rest of the day digging through the rubble, only to have it collapse on me all over again the next morning.

The pandemic took all of who I was at the beginning. I lay awake most nights, on top of already being awake for feedings with the baby or a nightmare my older son had, worrying for them constantly and just thinking how the hell am I going to survive another day inside this house with them? I know that my sons' brains are developing.

I know that when they are being little shits you are supposed to pause, validate their emotions and then, using play or fun, redirect them to a change of activity; I know all of that. However, when you are repeating yourself eight times over and have cleaned up the living room for the fourth time that day, you crack. There were moments that were so bad that I had to physically remove myself from the room to keep myself from ripping my own face off. Yes, Phyllis, I want to punch my kids in the face, sometimes. No, I don't hate my children, but they are irritating as hell. I know they can't control their emotions yet, but that doesn't mean it doesn't take its toll on me. I had no external resources during the pandemic. I am fortunate in that the boys have access to their grandparents, and as restrictions loosened, I allowed my parents to take my oldest, sometimes, because he and I very much needed a break from one another. Without that, though, I had nothing. There were no mom meet-ups at the library, which had sustained me in my first year of parenthood. There were no stroller fit classes, no swimming lessons, no baby-and-me activities. There was nothing to meet my needs, and yet I was expected to still be able to manage all the needs of my children.

I am well aware that I was not working during the bulk of the pandemic. I did have to teach online while my son was in junior kindergarten, though. The only way I was able to make it work was because my mother had boot camp training in Google Classroom and was able to navigate the day with him. There is no way I would have been able to have done my live high school lectures while corralling my four-year-old to learn through school (I am so very grateful to his teachers). While teaching online was truly not an experience that I have any desire to do again, the fact that I had a purpose outside of my home got me through, as opposed to on maternity leave when my entire existence was tied to home. I was allowed to exist as a person outside being a mother, and even though teaching during the pandemic was truly awful, that sense of purpose is what got me through. Had I had to do that for months on end, however, it would have been a very different experience. I do not know how a parent who was working and also navigating their young children's schoolwork coped for the entirety of the pandemic. I would not have made it. I know that. I would have returned down the black hole for a second round in the ring with depression, and I don't know that I would have won this time. Not having to work was my one saving grace during the pandemic. To those of you who had to do that and navigate children, I salute you completely.

The pandemic, for all its hideousness, amplified a lot of macabre whispers lurking in the shadows. It forced the things that were "just a part of being a parent" into the spotlight and shattered the dystopian reality of the modern expectations being placed on women in particular. Mothers are still expected to bear the brunt of the house and of their children. A lot of parents preferred to work from home because having no commute and being in the house allowed them to throw a load of laundry in or run out and do some errands during their lunch break. They were home when their kids got off the bus, so they didn't have to pay for after-school care. I say this as someone who has an equal partner in terms of household care and childcare, but let's be honest, the tabs of life are not flickering in his brain all night. Amidst all of this, as women, we are still supposed to be good at our jobs, maintain our bodies as if they had not been pulverized by our children (both in utero and out), be madly in love with our spouses and do it all with grace. I get it now. Those countless, abstract, terrifying stories that I read in university about suburban housewives in the 1950s who drowned their children. Rage. The most dangerous kind because it manifested behind pearls and a smile until it found its gruesome release.

When the rage had become consuming in that it was the main emotion I experienced all day almost every day, it was time to take control of that bitch. I let myself cry when my children were asleep because it was cathartic. And since I knew what my alternative storyline was from my first year of postpartum, I actively learned to outsmart my rage like maneuvers on a chess board. I did that by letting go. One pawn fell at a time. I was limited in the help that I could ask for outside of my home, but there were things I could control in my home, and I did so. We hired someone to clean our house twice a month after the lockdown lifted while I took my children outside or to my parents' house. I stopped spending my evenings looking up ridiculous, beautiful sensory bins to make for my son. He had a sandbox and was more than content to take his trucks in there for an hour.

We didn't learn all about the alphabet every day or do calendars. We went for walks and talked about the things he saw in the forest. I gave up on cooking completely. We ordered take-out once a week (sometimes, twice a week), and we basically ate some variation of the same ten meals or so on rotation. I let my older son start to watch movies when my younger one was napping, so I could sit on the couch next to him for an hour and do nothing. I was never worried about my kids being bored because boredom is a part of life, and to be honest, they are more creative for it, as they will find things to occupy themselves with. Boredom is critical for children. They need to learn that not every moment of their lives will be scheduled with entertainment for them. Some parts of life suck. Get used to it, kid.

Self-care has become the ultimate cliche of the

pandemic. I tried actively to invest in real self-care. Taking a shower or going to bed early or doing my writing were no longer rewards; I made them necessities. If a task was becoming overwhelming or irritating, I set it aside (sometimes, that task was being with my children, so I locked myself in the mudroom and canvassed social media for ten minutes while my husband was around). Going for a walk alone to listen to a podcast without my children became a regular fixture in my week. I started reading novels again. I watched *Bridgerton* and *Squid Game* (like every other basic human being on the planet), and the Duke of Hastings reminded me that there was beauty in the world outside of the walls of my confinement. If I felt like sitting on the couch for two hours and watching Netflix after they were in bed, I sat on my ass and did that. When I was given the opportunity to be away from my children, which was honestly not often, I relished in it. I blared my '90s playlist with my windows rolled down and my hoop earrings on and pretended I was driving to the airport like a naive 20-year-old who had a whole decade to herself still. I viewed my day in four segments: morning to nap time, naptime to dinner, dinner to bedtime and post-bedtime. If one sucked, I hung onto hope for the next one. I developed real coping mechanisms for myself, and if something impeded on those coping mechanisms, they were compartmentalized temporarily and dealt with when it was safe for me to do so. I often wonder if the horror that I went through the first time is what saved me during the pandemic. I stopped accepting that self-care is a privilege and demanded it be a necessity. I decided that whatever bullshit society had deemed as self-care for a mother was no longer going to be my definition of it. I had learned my strengths and weaknesses and knew when to call upon the first and when to respect the latter. I realized the problem wasn't me. It was the expectations I had placed on myself because I was viewing myself through the archetype that society had decided I needed to be.

The larger problem is that prior to the pandemic, parental rage existed. The pandemic just amplified it. Parents spend so much time wondering how much we can handle without properly assessing the collateral damage of doing so. Mothers can handle everything, can't we? Think of all the countless images you saw online during the pandemic of a mother working from home while breastfeeding and homeschooling her older children. Yes, they did it. That doesn't mean they should have to. Society and other women need to stop glorifying the image of burnout that has become motherhood. Posting about all the things you can do to show how superhuman you are contributes to the problem. I signed up for motherhood, not martyrdom. While the pandemic introduced extreme circumstances, which confined us to our homes, there are critical lessons that need to be taken away from that. Mothers need support in the modern-day village that looks different for everyone. For some of us, it is a nanny or day-care provider. Teachers, schools, day camps are all there, too. Part of my village is the team that comes and cleans my house for me. Our parents are part of our village, and we know how lucky we are to have them accessible to us in the same city. Take-out is very much a part of my village, and I love her. These resources need to be made available, especially affordable childcare. A parent should stay home with their children because they actively choose that, not because it is cheaper to keep one parent at home rather than providing society with accessible childcare.

I'm tired of being called a "supermom" or of people telling me, "I don't know how you do it!" I did it in the pandemic because I was in survival mode. I didn't have a choice. When this pandemic does end (nothing lasts forever), I have no intent of perpetuating the motherhood narrative that showcases me, a mom, as the "domestic goddess who also has a successful career while still being attractive and a fantastic mother." I am a person. Some days, I suck at my job, and other days, I suck at being a mother. Neither one of those is an accurate depiction of my existence in either role. They are snapshots of a larger canvas. Please stop striving to live up to this unrealistic expectation that is put on us. Doing so is part of the problem. If we feed into that narrative, it will never change because we are conditioning ourselves into the exact carica-ture that they want. We need to alter the narrative. If we do everything, society becomes complacent because they believe we can handle it. As soon as we stop, a disruption to people's lives emerges, and they become inconvenienced and notice it. Start saying no. It is my favourite word right now. Not "no, sorry I can't because …" or "no, sorry, I really want to but …" Just no. "No, I can't right now." That includes saying no to your spouse (my husband is well-adjusted to this), and it means saying no to your children.

The world that existed prior to Covid has been dismantled. It has been made clear that it was not sustainable. There were cracks in the foundation, and the pandemic simply exasperated complica-tions that were already there. What needs to hap-pen is that when we rebuild after the pandemic, as humans have been doing for thousands of years, we need to rebuild in a way that is meaningful. We need to rebuild a society that offers more balance. A society that still values hard work, but not ex-ploitation. A society that holds us accountable, but doesn't exonerate us of our choices and their con-sequences. A society where we are content with enough. The world will return to a version of pre-conceived normalcy, but it will never be the same. There has been too much loss to not alter our col-lective consciousness moving forward. You know what? I'm okay with that. We just have to be brave enough to shift from grasping at unrealistic expectations to pursuing meaningful ones.

Most importantly, and this is the one I struggled with the most, is learning how to say no to yourself. My brain never, *ever* shuts off, and I struggle with down time because I always feel like there is something else I can be doing. Even if I watch TV, a lot of times, I am multitasking with something else. I am working on it. I am learning to say, "no, that can wait until tomorrow," or "no, I can't take that on." I've never particularly struggled with saying no to others but am actively working on saying no to myself.

I still absolutely have moments of rage because my children continue to suck every ounce of my soul. I honestly don't know if I have one left. But when I feel my rage start to slither up my back, I can cut her off at the knees into retreat. I haven't managed to behead her yet and probably never will, but I look her straight in the eye now and remind her she has a time and place. Checkmate.

POPCORN

My son was given a marble race one Christmas. It's one of the only toys he has that I don't want to set on fire, because it occupies him for a significant amount of time. He can design racetracks in multiple configurations and loves it. While playing in the basement with it, he suddenly tore it to shreds one afternoon in frustration. When I asked what was wrong with it, he told me that Popcorn didn't like it.

I tried to summon all my parenting wisdom (it really doesn't take long, there isn't much) to process how I was going to handle the fact that my son had just invented a separate entity that lived in his head. I proceeded to ask why Popcorn didn't like it. He told me that the ramps were not working properly, so Popcorn told him that he had to redo it. I left it at that.

Slowly, over the next few weeks, Popcorn became a burgeoning figure in our family life. Whenever my son was told it was time to eat, he proceeded with adamant fervor that he was not required to eat because Popcorn told him he didn't have to. Apparently, Popcorn loves to eat vegetables, but my son doesn't. I was informed that it is okay for them to disagree on this. Without trying to be overbearing, but very much deliberate, I began my quest to get more information on this outlander. I asked my son what Popcorn looked like (as tall as me, evidently). I asked him if he sleeps in my son's room with him, and he said no, he sleeps in our guest room in the basement, which is also my husband's office. He prefers the basement. Apparently, Popcorn likes to hang out in my husband's office. My husband, terrified of ghosts, loathes this narrative. I think it's hilarious. My son frequently visits his dad at work and informs him that he needs to get off his computer because Popcorn needs to write an email to God knows who. Popcorn offers outfit suggestions to my son in the morning and eats whatever my son doesn't want at his meal ("don't worry, Mommy, Popcorn will eat it"). Popcorn also is clearly studying engineering because he proceeds to build obnoxious ramps and forts out of our couch cushions. I don't think he has left the house with us yet, but I am assuming that will shift shortly. Popcorn also has a very short temper and thinks that I am the meanest mommy in the world. Popcorn is an asshole. If I could find him without looking like an idiot, I would throat punch him.

At first, I didn't know what to make of Popcorn. I didn't immediately default to panic mode in concern that this meant that my son was mentally unstable by any means. Should Popcorn at any point instruct my son to hold a pillow over my face while I'm sleeping, we will seek out a professional. When I did some of my own research (that's fine for things like imaginary best friends, but probably not vaccines), I was reassured that having an imaginary best friend is a perfectly normal phase of development. It is often done as an act of defiance to take control. Children really don't have a lot of control over their own lives. To us, it's maddening ("no, you can't put rocks in the washing machine!"), but I imagine that to them, it must feel smothering at times. It made sense that my son, in coping with the loss of his version of normalcy, wearing masks, seeing much less people than we were used to and trying to learn how to make friends prior to starting school, would create a friend. I will give my son creativity points because Popcorn is a random, albeit sensational name for an imaginary friend. My imaginary friend's name was Jeremy. He disappeared or was kidnapped when I was about ten, I'm still not sure. I used to talk to him a lot when I was kid. I still talk to myself all the time.

I will catch glimpses of my son talking to himself. He is very expressive with his hands, the way I am, and he has a very expressive face. I imagine he is talking to Popcorn as they take on their latest crisis or how to potentially get out of something. I like it, for the most part. It means he creates worlds in his head. It means he can understand that there are people in the world who are different from him and that he can still get along with them. He also negotiates with Popcorn quite frequently. It is something I really enjoy about my son right now. It's awesome. For the foreseeable future, it looks like Popcorn will be a dedicated member of our family. As long as the knives are all in the drawer when I wake up in the morning, he's allowed to stay.

THE KIDS ARE ALRIGHT?

I think the first thing that most people, certainly myself, worried about when the pandemic started was how this was going to affect our children. My kids were not yet in school, so I didn't have the added worry of where they were at academically. I do know, however, that the first five years of a child's life are critical for the foundations that they will have for the rest of it. So, having those lost years within the first five years of both of my sons' lives weighed heavily on me. I know that with older children it would have likely been more difficult. Children who are older already have a social base. They have a group of friends or their sports team, and I have no doubt that the absence of those things would have caused mental strain. I don't know how they couldn't. I undoubtedly saw that strain in my teenage students. Some even resorted to cutting themselves. But what I was relieved to see was that even though the rates of children dealing with mental health issues were skyrocketing, we started to say that out loud. Parents and children were more open about having conversations around what was going on in their heads, and they tried to come up with strategies that allowed them to cope within the confines which they were allotted.

As a public-school teacher, I see the lack of mental health resources every day. Students are coming to school with issues that are way beyond the school's ability to handle, even though school boards will tell you that they are indeed a place for all. Saying that without having the resources in place, though, to create a safe space for all (staff and students) is a dangerous falsehood. Kids suffered during the pandemic, there is no argument there, but the beneficial change that did come out of it is that resources became available to them, and more importantly, they were willing to ask for help.

Right now, it doesn't seem like it, but the hope is that the open dialogue about mental health that has resulted from the pandemic will lead to productive, positive change. Resources are lacking, but that was true prior to the pandemic. We have seen, without argument, how those services are essential to a functioning society.

I also think we need to spend a heck of a lot more time building resilience in our children. People often say that "kids are so resilient," but are they innately resilient or is that just something we say? I don't think it is that kids are born resilient. I think they just care less about society's expectations of them, which is something that gets lost along the way into adulthood. I believe resilience is taught. I think, sometimes, it is forced on you because you don't know how strong you are until you are confronted with a circumstance that forces you to be. In speaking to my colleagues that taught during the beginning of the pandemic, they all said the same thing. There was a group of kids that no matter what you threw at them, they were able to figure it out. Then, there was another group that just crumbled. I'm not saying those kids should have just "kept calm and carried on." My god, at one point, I as an adult felt like I was trapped in *The Truman Show*. The question isn't a matter of why those kids were buckling. What the conversation needed to be was how are we going to teach them to get themselves through this?

Part of it is bolstering society's support for them. The other part comes down to parenting and teaching your children self-advocacy and that they can, and will be required to, do hard things in life. Does your child not know how to handle difficulty because you have never allowed them to? Think about that. In my career I have dealt with ample bulldozing and helicopter parents, and I can assure you, they are failing their children. I saw very clearly how the pandemic bolstered some of my students, and decimated others.

As the pandemic wanes, until it hopefully meets the agonizing end it deserves, this will get better. We will not emerge from this and snap back into life, but the support, the resources and the conversations that were had about our mental health during it need to continue. Kids are just surviving right now too, and that's okay. What matters more is what comes after for them. There will be an after, so what are we going to do with it? We can't pretend that their struggles just never happened. They need to be given the forum to talk about it, to process it, and to re-adjust to the world. That doesn't mean absolving them of responsibility, it means teaching them how to prioritize and compartmentalize. I have had multiple students tell me that they simply didn't have the time to get their work done (and ended up failing my class), but they always had time to have their lashes, nails and hair done. The world around these kids needs to shift, and that is not just within the framework of the people raising them, but also for those of us that are teaching them.

While the rest of the world was shifting to remote flexibility and listening to their employees about what they wanted on how to create more meaningful workplaces, teaching went in the exact opposite direction. Teachers will never have flexibility in our line of work. Yes, I get it, we get summer vacations off, spring break and two weeks at Christmas. Guess what? That is the collection of my lieu time for the hours of planning and marking that I do while I'm not at work. Coach a sports team? Run a club? There is no extra pay or time compensation for that.

We were required to show compassion and understanding to our students and meet them where they were. Little of that compassion was shown to us, however. We were required to pull off teaching remotely and back to in-person in a mere day's notice. Parents were frustrated, and rightly so, by the back and forth as well. They took it out on us, even though teachers have absolutely NO SAY in the day-to-day operations of our school boards. Believe me, if we did, our schools would run much more efficiently. We are the foot soldiers, the disposables, and no one talked to us about what we needed to make it through teaching in the pandemic. Instead, we were told to do yoga or go for walks. This was often communicated to us in staff meetings that could have been an email. We were forced to do busy work about school improvement when all we desperately needed to do was survive the pandemic.

I understand the value and importance of my job, but we go through divorces, struggle with infertility, lose children, take care of parents or spouses that are terminally ill, and we have our own health struggles. We are human. Please stop defining us by the one-dimension of our profession. We are an entire being. If we too are depleted we can't be who we need to be in the classroom for your children.

I am your child's teacher. I am also the daughter of immigrants who fled dictatorship and poverty. I am the wife of a refugee who fled a bloody civil war. I am the daughter-in-law of a woman who needed to wave a white baby blanket out of the car to cross into an occupied city just to get to a hospital to deliver her baby. I am the mother of children who are first-generation Canadians, and they will understand what that means, both the good and the bad. I am your child's teacher—a fully-formed, flawed human being. Please remember that.

In terms of watching my own sons get through

this, the thing that stood out to me the most was how completely parallel their development was, even though my older son had been exposed to a normal world and my youngest had no idea what the world was. Both rolled at six months. My oldest crawled at nine months and my second at eight (but that kid had a head start because he was the second child who lived on the floor). They both said their first clear, distinctive word shortly before 12 months. And they both walked at 14 months. My oldest son went to a one-nap toddler schedule at 14 months; my youngest did it at 15 months. Shortly before both of their second birthdays, they were speaking in two-to-three-word sentences.

The argument that pandemic babies will be behind is not a theory I endorse, especially when you read the studies. Most of the researchers were wearing masks for the short time frame that the studies were being conducted. Of course, the results would look worrisome. Babies need facial expressions as cues. They were not getting that from the researchers, but they were getting that from their families. I realized that even though the world was on fire outside my house, my children were going to be okay because their primary agent of socialization (myself and my husband) were solid. Not on the inside, but we did everything we could to provide them with some semblance of routine and normality, even though there was nothing normal about it.

In watching children at my neighbourhood park, I am happy to see how quickly their faces light up when they see another child. How eager they are to climb the monkey bars or try a new slide. I know parents are worried for their children, myself included, but I remind myself that I have taught numerous students (both children and adults) who have fled their countries due to poverty, hunger, oppression. My first teaching job was teaching English to new immigrants. Through that role I met people who spent their formative years living in a tent in a refugee camp. Don't tell me that because your kid couldn't play soccer for a year that their entire prospects have been denied to them. You couldn't possibly be that ignorant. In time, kids will return to being kids. Regular sports and clubs will return, and a regular classroom will return.

I am cautious to subscribe to the notion that our children will be the pandemic's permanent collateral damage. I often think of my grandmother who used to save cooking oil to reuse it. I always found that strange as a kid. It wasn't until I got older that I realized she did it because she had grown up poor and learned not to waste things. Growing up in the Great Depression inevitably shaped my grandmother, in the way that this pandemic will shape our children, but it didn't dominate my grandmother's entire adult existence.

Our kids learned to appreciate things more, including their education, because for the first time in a lot of their lives, things were taken away from them. They learned how to wait in line and that not everything was going to be instantaneous anymore. They learned that the things they do and the choices they make affect other people. Some saw selfishness and paid the price of their parents' ignorance. Some learned selflessness and collective responsibility. May we look at the reckoning that this pandemic has been for anyone who is not the heteronormative white male.

The kids are not going to be okay today or tomorrow. They deserve to mourn the milestones of their youth. Don't dismiss that for them, but continue to hold them accountable to their future. Even if they don't understand it now, that is a way to show them they are loved regardless of what is happening in the world. It is going to take time, it is going to take hard work, love and a lot of forgiveness, but the kids *will be* alright.

We should probably get on climate change though.

KINDERGARTEN

I, like any parent, was worried about my son starting kindergarten. I was more worried because he was supposed to go to pre-school but didn't end up going because of Covid. I tried to do my best to get him ready at home, but I'm not a kindergarten teacher for a reason, and there is no substitute for playing with other children. My son was the first grandchild in both families. He didn't have any immediate cousins. He has always been comfortable with adults and older children but is extremely shy around children his own age. When we are at the park, he will be hesitant to introduce himself to another child but will have absolutely no problem talking up the child's mom. I did what I could by driving him past his school. We got out a few times and walked around the kindergarten yard, so he could see where he would be dropped off in the morning and where he would be picked up.

I don't know if there is anything more terrifying than handing off your child that first day of school. They are still so little, but not really. I worry constantly if I did enough to get him ready, to help him feel safe and secure. I remind myself that, despite what some parents think, no kindergarten teacher is going to look out into the little faces in front of them and be able to point out which ones were breastfed, which ones were formula-fed and which ones were sleep-trained as opposed to co-sleeping. There is no elite blue mat or relegated red mat for the children to sit on depending on your parental choices. The teacher doesn't care if your kid can count to 100 but can't put on his own shoes. They will not be impressed by party tricks. I tried to worry less about getting my son ready academically and, instead, focused on giving him tools that would allow him to be independent. Getting him to open and close his own backpack. Putting on his own shoes and jacket (sometimes, he still needs help with his zipper). We practiced opening his water bottle and lunch box. I did what I could to make my son capable of independence. And I trust his teacher to start off his academic learning with support from us at home.

On the first day of school, my husband dropped my son off. The thing with teaching is that because you are required to be the purveyor of other children's milestones, you so often miss out on many of your own child's. My husband sent me a video of my little guy walking up to his teacher—stiff upper lip and not turning around once. When I went to pick him up after his first day, I could tell as soon as he came out of the door that he was upset. When I asked how his day was, he simply said he missed me and didn't like school all that much because it was too much time away from me. I felt relieved to know that I hadn't screwed him up and that he did indeed miss me, but it also hurt that this was his first experience away from me. The guilt came crashing in. I hadn't made the right choice by keeping him out of pre-school. I was trying to protect him and his baby brother from a virus, and no matter what I did, I always felt like I was making the wrong choice. But then, I remind myself that his development mentally, socially and emotionally cannot just come from me. I will not be with him forever. If that is the case, then I failed as a parent. My job is to teach and then allow for independence that is earned. He needs to work with other people, he needs to learn that he does not always get what he wants, and he needs to learn that his actions have consequences for others. My husband and I went back and forth about whether we were going to send him during the pandemic. And the weight of protecting him from a virus while weighing everything else he missed out on ravaged my brain. We knew we couldn't keep him locked in his ivory tower until the princess (or prince) came to save him. He was going to have to return to life at some point, and for us, that point was school. He might not be able to do everything, but he was going to school.

There is always the nerve-racking aspect or question of "will my child be able to make friends?" My sons are both natural observers. My oldest son, even as a baby, was never the kid who lunged at the pile of toys that had been dumped on the floor during the library program. He was more than content to sit in my lap and watch the other children play. He loved going to coffee shops where he would just sit in his stroller and watch people come and go. My second son is largely the same. He will generally just watch people, unless he sees that you have French fries, at which point, he will promptly invade your personal space and stick out his hand, begging for one.

I remember being at a splash pad one summer, and

a mother was watching her daughter run through it. She kept telling the other woman she was with that her daughter will change the world. I watched the kid repeatedly get hit in the face with the same spout. She was next to my son who was trying to drink the water.

I am all for validating your children. When my son builds a block tower, I don't kick it over and say, "do it again, child." I feign interest and tell him it is wonderful, even though it is basic AF. The difference here is that I acknowledged my son for doing something. This whole mentality of telling children that they will change the world simply for existing, for gracing the rest of us, mortals, with their presence here on earth is dangerous. If your three-year-old speaks five languages fluently and can play the harpsichord, then sure, you can probably say that child will do great things. But this mentality of telling children they are great all the time that is not attached to an action is more harmful than helpful as far as I am concerned as an educator.

That child becomes the teenager who loses it when he is failing after doing nothing. That child has the potential to become a university student whose parent calls my best friend, a professor of infectious diseases, to tell her that her kid needs his midterm date changed because he wants to go away with his friends for the weekend (true story).

That kid becomes the adult who will call, asking for a three day bereavement because his hamster died (also a true story). This is not an easy change of thinking in the context of modern parenting where we feel like we must compensate for the mistakes of previous generations (I am all for no longer smoking and drinking during pregnancy or striking your child with a belt), but I feel like neglecting everything that previous generations did is insulting. I want my sons to cry when they are sad. I want them to know that it is okay as a male to be afraid, vulnerable and kind. However, maybe we have gone too far the other way? I am working on this myself. I, by default, often say, "hello, my beautiful boys," when I see them in the morning. I am actively trying to stop doing this and, instead, attach verbs to them. For example, I will say, "hello, my kind boy." And I do this so that they learn that I am acknowledging and applauding them for choices that they make and actions that they undertake as opposed to things they simply are. Of course, I think that my children are beautiful. They are mine. But I would be remiss in believing that constantly telling them that they're beautiful is going to prepare them for adulthood. Moral of the story: should you hang your kid's shitty artwork on the fridge when they bring it home from school? Yes, because they made something and that's important. Should you tell him that he will be the next Michelangelo because he finger painted something that resembles a crime scene? Probably not.

There is a worry that doing so might just result in a kid who is so angry at the world because he was supposed to do great things and be a great someone simply for existing, without putting in any of the hard work that goes behind greatness. Please note that when I say "great," I am not talking about people whose sole ambition is to collect a social media following. I am talking about the people who change policy, those who get up and go to save lives every day, those who get people out of abusive relationships and families, those who help new immigrants find homes and those who prepare school lunches for children who don't have one. I am talking about people who share their vulnerability to make others feel less alone. People who make real, tangible change in the world they touch. I don't want that perceived greatness (that is not backed by action) to become the flaw in my child's life that means he and Popcorn will still be living with me as adults. That starts by me letting go and trusting the world will catch him. If it doesn't, then he is going to learn how to climb the hell out of where he was swallowed. For me, building that resilience started in pandemic kindergarten.

SLIDING DOORS

I f there is one thing that I am tired of hearing, it is parents trying to climatize their parenting experience to parenting little children in a pandemic. The collective trauma of parenting little ones during this time can only be understood by those of us who endured it. I'm not saying that other generations of parents have not suffered. I teach history. I make it abundantly clear to my students that we are not the first generation who has suffered, and we will not be the last. I have no understanding of what it is like to parent while saying goodbye to my husband who is off to war. I don't know what it is like to frantically grab my children and run underground into the subway while bombs decimate the world as I know it above me. Nor do I have any comprehension of what it is like to flee on foot with a baby strapped to my back to cross a fabricated border where I am persecuted on one side and given asylum on the other.

I often think of my grandparents, all born in the 1930s, entering the world years into the Great Depression. They spent their childhoods living in World War II. They then spent their teenage years and their twenties living under a dictatorship before deciding to leave the only island they had ever known in their thirties, all to protect their sons from military conscription on their fourteenth birthdays. I can't imagine the frantic, hushed conversations my grandparents had in the middle of the night, deciding whether to uproot their children to a country so unlike the only world they had ever known. Leaving a tiny island in the middle of the Atlantic Ocean to move to the second biggest, second most frigid country in the world was a harrowing decision, I imagine. I cannot empathize with these individuals or my grandparents, but what is communal between our shared experiences is human suffering. There are degrees of suffering, of course. I would never claim that being figuratively locked inside my house is the same as giving birth inside of a bomb shelter. I have lived a life of safety and privilege. I have lived a life that many around the world dream of. A life that parents seek for the children that they desperately place in a boat because the treacherous water provides them with the opportunity of hope that the land has long since denied them. A life that is so commonplace to many of us that we have lost touch on just how privileged we are.

What we can do for each other is acknowledge that parents who have survived this have suffered. Yes, we signed up to be parents. We did not sign up to parent during a pandemic. We are allowed to struggle, to be angry, to feel engulfed by a deepening pit of despair as the days, weeks and months have all rolled into one unrelenting yearslong nightmare. Especially for those of us who had children in the last age group to be vaccinated, or for parents with immunocompromised children. Most importantly, we are allowed to mourn this lost time. We have mourned the loss of milestones and the ability to make memories within childhood, which is a finite entity. So, if you did not parent during this pandemic, yes, it was likely hard for you, too, and yes, you likely suffered through parenthood in your own way, but you do not understand this brand of parenting struggle. Please stop telling me that you do. That would be like me claiming to understand the decision my grandparents made. I don't.

I have made peace with the fact that in this pandemic I have not been a bad mom. I absolutely have bad moments and bad days when I fail unequivocally. I have moments I am ashamed of. I yelled at my children, grabbed them by the arm, ignored them. There were so many nights during the pandemic when I would quietly enter my sons' rooms when they were asleep and gently kiss their foreheads to silently murmur an apology and beg their forgiveness for my failures that day. I also reminded them that they had been quite terrible.

I worry like every parent, but I desperately try to convince myself that the imposing trauma of this pandemic can be utilized to serve a higher purpose. I think it allowed us to see people for who they truly were and whether they took our shared responsibility to one another seriously. It showed an ugly selfishness in some who prioritized their own convenience over people's lives. It unleashed a deafening truth to all of us about what mattered in life and what didn't. It allowed us to see the true cost of ignorance, which in this case, cost people their lives. We can choose who is and is not in our lives moving forward because they said or did things that we can never unsee. There are some things that don't deserve to be forgiven. It doesn't matter if you are family or if we were friends; I can be ashamed of you and do not have to justify no longer wanting a relationship with you. That is called self-preservation, and it is essential to my existence as a mother. That is not the same as cancelling all people who challenge you and tell you the truth when you don't want to hear it.

I often wonder about what my sons will think when they are old enough to learn about this period in history. Will my older son remember masks? Will he remember being stuck at home so often? Will he remember me screaming at him or crying on the floor because that day was just too heavy? Did I break them? Will my baby have hidden scars from this that won't manifest for ten years? I don't know, but I don't think so. I do know that during a global health crisis, when I was constantly trying to outrun the demons nipping at my heels that had plagued me during my first postpartum period, I was good enough. My sons were kept safe, they were cared for, and above everything, they were loved. Even if they are too young to understand that, my husband and I did everything we could to protect them. We were vaccinated to protect ourselves and them because it was our responsibility to do so. We were their armor. I mean, not dying is also high up on my list of reasons for getting vaccinated, but I'm going to go with the sentimental parental moment here. We became selective about who was in our children's lives and will continue with that practice moving forward. You do not owe people anything when it comes to your children. You are their guardians. You get to decide who will be beneficial to their lives and who won't. Do not apologize for that.

There will be a collective trauma from this period that will be processed by different people in different ways. Some will re-emerge back into life instantaneously and without hesitation. Many others will continue to have reservations, to which they are entitled. I for one will no longer use public transit or sit in an auditorium without a mask. I don't know how my children will come out of this. Part of me thinks that they will be so eager to return to normal that these lost years won't matter. Another part of me thinks that my oldest will be hesitant when meeting new people and will not know a world without sanitizer checkpoints (I mean, not a bad thing). I don't know how I will come out of this. I am riddled with scars from my first time as a parent, and those gashes were slashed deeper and wider during the pandemic, but I have learned to wear that scar tissue proudly. I own them, and in refusing to apologize for their ugliness, they cannot be used against me. The bottom line is that I just want my children to be okay. What if we pivoted from the lofty idealizations we fabricate for our children to the desire for them to just be okay as functioning human beings, instead? Maybe the world would be a little less terrible.

What I am proud of is to be a part of the revolution that is currently underway in parenthood. It is not an overnight coup with blood coursing through the cobblestone streets. It is an insidious revolution, one that begins in whispers from one person to another, daring to speak the truth. The frustration, the failures, the anger, the regrets and the loneliness. The facade of pious motherhood martyrdom is slowly being chipped away, and it's exhilarating.

EPILOGUE

Dear Boys,

Ultimately, I don't know. Isn't there something so liberating in admitting that? I still don't know what I'm doing as your mom, and I don't know what parenting in a post-pandemic world looks like. What I do know is that we will come out of this, and when we do, we will never forget that we did just that. We got out. Ambivalence is at the core of humanity. We are simultaneously merciless and compassionate, brave and fearful, intelligent and ignorant. Think of all the ugliness, all the terror that the world has forced on us and the destruction humanity has forced on itself. But we keep living anyway.

When you learn about what you didn't remember you will learn of the hate and ugliness of this time. Acknowledge it. Learn from it. But don't give those people more time than they deserve. Instead, look for the ordinary people that saved us. Being ordinary does not hinder the opportunity to do extraordinary things. If you grow up to be just that, an ordinary person who is creating good in the world, I have done my job.

All I can hope for you is that the new world that is forged in the ashes of the pandemic provides the foundation for a better world for you and all pandemic babies. There is no guarantee of this, and that uncertainty haunts my restless dreams. I mean, it's a long shot, because people are the worst, but never underestimate the audacity of hope.

She can be quite cruel, but she is loyal, and she occupies the space she is entitled to. I'll take my chances with her and with you.

Love,

Mom

ACKNOWLEDGE-
MENTS

Thank you to Chunk for being my pandemic buddy, and for being the sweetest, snuggliest little guy ever. Also, thank you for sleeping.

Pompochino, for driving me to limits I didn't know I was capable of, both good and bad. These books would not have existed without your absurd choices of what is offending you at any particular moment.

To my husband for reading the first draft and your tweaks. More importantly, thank you for purchasing our sink caddy.

To Jennifer, my editor and illustrator who takes random ideas in my head and makes them exist in the world.

To Joe and Ines. Again, thanks for not considering abandonment. Especially through years two to five.

To all the parents of pandemic babies. I see you. I am you.

Our babies are going to be okay.

ABOUT THE AUTHOR

Nicole Correia

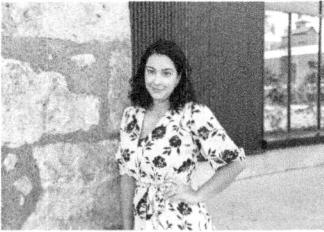

Nicole Correia is a high school teacher who lives in Ontario, Canada. She survives on copious amounts of chocolate that she eats with the fridge door open so that her children will not see her and interupt her five minutes of peace. She does not mince words when it comes to mother-hood, and encourages others to do the same.

BOOKS BY THIS AUTHOR

Push

If you are looking for a heart-warming story about the joys of becoming a parent, this is not that book. It is probably not a great shower gift idea, either. This is more of a showing up with a meal and copious amounts of coffee after the baby is born kind of gift. When a baby is born to a mother her entire world, for better or worse, is shattered overnight. The truth about that destruction is the story you will find here. Shattered pieces can be lacquered back together though, and even if the piece is never quite the same, it is still worthy.

PRAISE FOR AUTHOR

"I have never related to a book more in my life! This book is short, sweet, relatable and best of all hilarious. It was like someone finally understood how I felt! If you are a mom looking for a good quick read this is it!"

"What Nicole has done is written a book that will not only give you an up close and personal look into pregnancy and motherhood, but will also help women feel like they're not alone. The language and words she uses in her book help you really understand what a women is thinking and feeling in those exact moments. By being so transparent she is paving the way for other women to speak out and ask for help if they need it. Having four sisters and almost having a baby of my own, I can tell you that what Nicole has beautifully written is not for the faint of heart. It is real, it is brutally honest and all husbands, boyfriends, uncles, brothers and all men really, need to read this book. She is reminding us to be kinder to ourselves and to

each other- and honestly, the next time you see a tired mom, smile at her, it might just make her day."

"Nicole's account of the first year of motherhood brought me to tears--both from laughter and empathy. Her voice is filled with wit and vulnerability, which any mother will appreciate. She raises very important points about modern-day motherhood, compels us to recognize the true challenges, and calls us to respect mothers--regardless of what they have to do to survive and PUSH through that crazy first year!"

"Very refreshing to hear the honest take from a new Mom. Too many hide the truth or sugar coat their experience. That does not help other new Mom's to be prepared for what's ahead of them. This will help Mom's to see that it's OK and they are not alone. I would have loved to have this book before I became a Mom."

"I wish I had this book when I first gave birth to my daughter. I couldn't put it down. It's real. It's raw. It's what I wanted (and needed) to read during such a stressful time. A big thank you to the writer for sharing her story. Highly recommend!"

"Whether you want to have kids or already have kids, you were pushed out of someone at some point. Nicole provides an incredibly honest reflection on the pregnancy, birth, and postpartum experience. Your mom definitely deserves some flowers and a large bottle of wine for all she went through. I have so much respect for anyone who goes through the pregnancy and child raising experience, especially Nicole!"

"Push is a book that sums up so honestly the struggles of pregnancy, child birth, and the early months of motherhood while also being very funny and light-hearted. Once I started reading I couldn't put it down. A great read for all mothers especially those still trying to keep their heads above water each day."

WHAT YOU WON'T REMEMBER

Made in the USA
Las Vegas, NV
10 April 2022